S0-ATI-119

Henry David Thoreau   Mark Twain   Carl Van Doren   G.K.Chester

Points of View   Theodore Dreiser

Hilaire Belloc   Irwin Edman   Bruce Hutchison   A.G.Gardiner

GENERAL EDITOR: *Dr. Earl W. Buxton, University of Alberta, Edmonton*

ASSISTANT EDITORS: *Mr. James Bell, University of Alberta, Edmonton*
Mr. Cyril Groves, Western Canada High School, Calgary
Mr. Rod Morisset, University of Calgary, Calgary
Sister Margaret Rose, O'Leary High School, Edmonton
Miss Marion Staples, Ross Sheppard High School, Edmonton

gage PUBLISHING LIMITED
TORONTO ONTARIO CANADA

Robertson Davies　　　Charles Lamb　　　William Hazlitt　　　Corey F

Eric Nicol　　Philip Wylie　　E.B.White　　Joyce Cary　　Randolph Bor

Solomon E.Asch　　Aldous Huxley　　William Faulkner　　J.B.Pries

Michel de Montaigne   Francis Bacon   John Donne   Richard Steele

Joseph Addison   Samuel Johnson   James Boswell   Henry David

Acknowledgments   Abraham Lincoln   John Ruskin

The editors of this anthology gratefully acknowledge the help of the teachers who worked with them in the experimental program which was designed to test the content of this text in a variety of classroom situations and determine its suitability for a senior matriculation class. The valuable comments and contributions made by Mrs. Irene Hargreaves, Mr. Earl Hawkesworth, Mr. Ronald Hirsch, Mr. Cedric Jewell, and Mrs. Edith Russell are appreciated.

We are grateful also to the various authors and publishers who have permitted the use of their work. Every attempt has been made to trace the owners of copyrighted material and make the proper acknowledgment with each selection. Should any error in acknowledgment have inadvertently crept in, we would be happy to make the appropriate correction in our next printing.

— the editors

A NOTE ON STYLE *We have attempted in each case to reproduce the text of the original; hence there will be discrepancies in spelling and punctuation, which vary with the times and depend also on the usage of the author's country of origin.*

Solomon E. Asch   Aldous Huxley   Corey Ford   Robertson Davies

J. B. Priestley   Philip Wylie   Hugh MacLennan   Samuel Johnson

nes Boswell   Abraham Lincoln   William Hazlitt   Charles Lamb

Introduction

This book contains forty-three essays selected to provide basic materials
for the non-fiction part of a literature course for high school seniors. The
decisions as to which essays were to be included out of the thousands
available were made by a group of high-school teachers at the conclusion
of an experimental program in which these and other essays were read
and discussed by matriculation students in rural and urban grade twelve
classes. The essays and, in some instances, selections from longer works,
finally chosen for this anthology were those that the majority of the
teachers found most effective in engaging students' interest, widening their
understanding of man and society, provoking spirited discussion, and
providing stimulating topics for writing.

The essays included in the anthology as a result of this process are
representative of literary periods from the sixteenth century to the present.
We have called the book *Points of View* because each essayist has selected
his own vantage point from which to observe whatever conventions,
institutions, beliefs, or kinds of behavior he thinks worth discussing. Often
the point of view of a writer causes him to reach conclusions quite
different from those that might be called conventional. To illustrate:
Thoreau considers the post office and newspapers something of a menace;
Charles Lamb sees merit in taking recreation—for example gambling—
seriously; Philip Wylie's comments on the education of young people
would undoubtedly get vigorous opposition from anyone concerned
with public safety.

On some subjects the writers do not agree with each other. For example,
both Samuel Johnson and Theodore Dreiser experienced poverty as a
long prelude to success, but their conclusions concerning its advantages and
limitations are not the same. Thoreau and Mark Twain found
contentment and inspiration in the country, whereas Charles Lamb was
unimpressed by the beauty of nature.

James Boswell   William Hazlitt   Charles Lamb   Abraham Linc̶

Ruskin·   Henry David Thoreau   Mark Twain   Carl Van Doren

G.K.Chesterton   Hilaire Belloc   Theodore Dreiser   Irwin Edmar

The diversity among the essays is not confined to subject and point of view, for the selections also vary widely in form, purpose, tone, mood, structure, and style. A brief comparison of a few of the selections may illustrate this diversity and suggest implications for study and discussion.

The first two essays in this anthology were written by Montaigne, the founder of the personal essay, almost four hundred years ago. In his introductory remarks to the reader, Montaigne said that he wrote "to the private convenience of my relatives and friends . . . in my simple, natural, ordinary fashion, without straining or artifice; for it is myself I portray."

The essays by Bacon, one of Montaigne's most enthusiastic readers, reveal both similarities and differences in purpose and style. Though Bacon portrays something of himself — for example, his intelligence and erudition — his essays on studies and marriage reveal much of the "artifice and constraint" that Montaigne sought to avoid. Bacon's conscious art is evident in his deliberately intriguing opening sentences, his use of balance and parallelism, his metaphors and classical quotations, and his terse aphorisms and admonitions. His intention was both to entertain and to give his reader a distillation of the knowledge he had gained from a classical education, from wide reading, and from his close observation of men and affairs.

In sharp contrast to Montaigne's placidity and Bacon's gravity is Hazlitt's irascibility in "On The Ignorance of the Learned." In portraying himself, Hazlitt reveals a man emotionally involved in his subject — a man who uses the essay as a medium not only to present his arguments but to vent his wrath against an educational system and its useless products. His long paragraphs are packed with generalizations and illustrations, metaphor and hyperbole, contrast and paradox, all designed to convince his readers that those who have "passed through the regular gradations of a classical education" are "mere literary drudges," devoid of ideas, commonsense, and sensitivity to the world of nature and of man.

In a senior class Hazlitt's essay can be "chewed and digested," analyzed critically, and discussed vigorously, because Hazlitt communicates not only ideas but feeling; his essay will have its staunch defenders and its incensed opponents. In many of the experimental classes, teachers found an almost equally vigorous response to the essays of other writers who attack our customs and institutions: the excerpt from Thoreau's *Walden*, Wylie's "Safe and Insane," and Edman's "On American Leisure" can be disruptive of class tranquility.

To restore harmony, the teacher may need to turn to Addison's good-humored ridicule of ladies' fans and head-dresses, Benchley's pseudo-serious "Talk to Young Men" about the Facts of Life, or Eric Nichol's "Love Affair" with his new automobile. In purpose, tone, and treatment these essays are different from those of Hazlitt, Thoreau, and Wylie — and they are also different from each other. For example, Addison is poking fun at the behavior of other people; Benchley is parodying the address of the guest lecturer or graduation speaker; and Nicol, in describing his "terror of the first scratch" on his new automobile, is portraying himself as the prototype for all of us who have parted with our old car and a substantial sum of money so that we may experience "the surge of power" underneath that "lovely burgundy body."

It is evident that the manner in which a writer presents his ideas depends not only upon his purpose but upon the time and place in which he is writing and the readers to whom he is addressing his remarks. For example, Bacon did not hesitate to use Latin quotations or classical allusions, because he was writing for the small proportion of the British population who had been privileged to attend the "public schools" where they began the study of the classics at the age of six or seven and followed a

Bacon   John Donne   Eric Nicol   Richard Steele   Joseph Addison

Samuel Johnson   Abraham Lincoln   John Ruskin   James Boswell

William Hazlitt   Charles Lamb   Henry David Thoreau

curriculum largely devoted to translating Latin works and writing Greek epigrams. A century later, Addison and Steele were producing their newspaper for an audience not so limited as that of Bacon: their most enthusiastic readers were the members of a rapidly expanding "middle class" that included doctors, writers, politicians, and businessmen, who gathered in the London coffee houses to discuss the latest issue of *The Tatler* and *The Spectator* along with other news of the day. Students may wish to compare Bacon's or Addison's style with that of Randolph Bourne who wrote for literary magazines, that of Edman and Colby who contributed to *Harper's* and the *Atlantic*, or that of Eric Nicol whose daily column is designed to provide hundreds of thousands of contemporary newspaper readers with comic relief from the daily disturbing reports of inflation, strikes, taxes, wars, and rumors of war.

Among these and the other essays there are differences in form and structure as well as in style. The student who has devoted any time to a discussion of newspapers will have no difficulty explaining the differences between the structure and arrangement of Eric Nicol's paragraphs and those of writers like Hazlitt and Thoreau. The essay form in which Solomon Asch discusses "Opinions and Social Pressure" is quite different from Robertson Davies' series of entries from "The Diary of Samuel Marchbanks," because these two writers have different purposes. Asch is describing certain kinds of human behavior observed under carefully controlled conditions. His essay is a scientific report, organized in terms of problem, procedures, conclusions, and implications. Each of Robertson Davies' essays is a single paragraph, and most of the paragraphs are structured in the same way: the writer first mentions an observation or experience, then analyzes it briefly, and finally presents a conclusion concerning its meaning or its effects upon his attitude or behavior.

This variety of content and treatment should give the teacher freedom in selecting teaching procedures and material that will be of interest to his

class. For example, some teachers may wish to use a chronological
approach, selecting representative essays from each period and encouraging
the class to examine and discuss differences in content, structure, and
style that are related to both the personality of the writer and the social
and intellectual milieu in which his work was created. Other teachers
may find that a topical or thematic approach is practicable, because
certain topics and themes are recurrent. For example, Boswell, Belloc, and
Dreiser are concerned with the results of poverty, but they differ in point
of view and method of treatment. Bacon, Hazlitt, Lincoln, Priestley, and
Wylie all have something to say about education. Other essays may be
grouped under such topics as "The Meaning of Leisure," "The Pursuit of
Status," or "Changing Fashions in Society." Sometimes a discussion of
two or three essays can be related to current problems. For example,
newspaper editorials on the purposes and costs of education are of frequent
occurrence and may serve as an introduction to "Of Studies" and "The
Ignorance of the Learned"; current arguments concerning the age at
which young people should be licensed to drive motor scooters or
automobiles are related to Wylie's "Safe and Insane"; the essays by Lamb,
Thoreau, Mark Twain, White, and MacLennan can be relevant to class
discussions of Romantic poetry or to articles on urbanization or the
complexity of modern life. MacLennan contrasts the prevailing attitudes
of the twentieth century with those of the eighteenth and considers the
implications for the artist.

In addition to encouraging close reading, critical thinking, and class
discussion, the essays should provide numerous and varied approaches to
the correlation of literature and composition. Today there is a growing body
of research which indicates that the effective writer is one who has read
widely and has consciously or subconsciously "got into [his] bones the
essential structure of the ordinary British sentence" — which, in the
words of Winston Churchill, "is a noble thing." Hans Guth states the

principle in this way: "If instruction in rhetoric is to bear fruit, the student must see the strategies and devices of good prose at work in a wide variety of reading, assigned and unassigned."[1]

The "strategies and devices" that Guth has in mind include the ways in which a writer records observations, supports his arguments, organizes his material, and exploits the resources of language — its sentence structure and vocabulary — to achieve clarity and force. Though the student's first task in his study of literature is discovering what the writer says and perhaps what he implies, there is also a place for some examination of the relationship between form and content, between what a writer says and how he has chosen to say it. In analyzing a writer's style or in comparing the organization, tone, sentence structure, prose rhythm, and illustrative devices used by a writer like Bacon with those of Steele, Hazlitt, or Ford, the student can increase his awareness of the flexibility and power of his own language. An increasing awareness may help him to use the resources of language more effectively.

Because every good essayist is both a competent writer and a perceptive observer, the study of a variety of essays should help a student to recognize that almost any experience, real or vicarious, can provide material for writing. The effectiveness of the essay that results from the experience will depend upon two qualities in the writer. The first is his ability to select the elements of the experience that may be meaningful and interesting to his reader. The second is a sensitivity to language that will enable him to select the words and arrangements of words that best communicate his meaning, his feeling, and something of his personality. Endowed with these qualties, by nature or by training or by both, the writers whose work appears in this anthology have created interesting essays on such apparently dull subjects as ladies' fans, report cards, whist, income tax

[1] *quoted from Hans Guth, <u>English for Today and Tomorrow</u>, Englewood Cliffs, N.J., 1964, p. 173*

returns, petticoats, and time. The student may not find these particular topics suitable for his own writing, but the essays can show him how a good writer observes, reflects on his observation, selects the elements which are interesting to him, and then finds the kind of language that will record the glimpse of life that he feels worth preserving.

Because the essays in *Points of View* are representative of diverse times, places, literary conventions, and points of view, some of them are sufficiently difficult to demand close, patient reading before they surrender their full meaning and implications. We believe that senior students in a matriculation program are prepared to exert this kind of effort, because it can help them to develop an awareness of the vitality and flexibility of their language. The English we use today has achieved its richness and adaptability because speakers and writers through the centuries have been investigators and innovators, constantly searching for the words and the sentence patterns that will communicate their thoughts and feelings with grace and precision.

In summary, we hope that the varied materials in this anthology will provide interesting reading, increase students' appreciation of their language, and stimulate them to understand and to consider ideas and points of view that may be at variance with their own.

reau   # Contents   *Frank Moore Colby   Robert Benchley*

Montaigne, who has been called the founder of the personal essay, was born at Dordogne, France. After receiving a very thorough classical education at home under the guidance of his father, he graduated from the Collège de Guyenne at Bordeaux and then studied law. For some time he was counsellor-at-law in the Parlement of Bordeaux, but at the age of thirty-eight he retired to devote all his time to writing and contemplation. In 1581 he was called from this quiet life to become mayor of Bordeaux, a position which he held for two terms.

To the two volumes of writings which appeared in 1580, he gave the name Essais,

(1533-1592)

**MICHEL
de MONTAIGNE**

meaning "attempts" to "speak unto paper as to the first man I meet" his reflections on man and society. The first complete edition of the Essays *was published in 1595, three years after Montaigne's death.*

To the Reader

This book was written in good faith, reader. It warns you from the outset that in it I have set myself no goal but a domestic and private one. I have had no thought of serving either you or my own glory. My powers are inadequate for such a purpose. I have dedicated it to the private convenience of my relatives and friends, so that when they have lost me (as soon they must), they may recover here some features of my habits and temperament, and by this means keep the knowledge they have had of me more complete and alive.

If I had written to seek the world's favor, I should have bedecked myself better, and should present myself in a studied posture. I want to be seen here in my simple, natural, ordinary fashion, without straining or artifice; for it is myself that I portray. My defects will here be read to the life, and also my natural form, as far as respect for the public has allowed. Had I been placed among those nations which are said to live still in the sweet freedom of nature's first laws, I assure you I should very gladly have portrayed myself here entire and wholly naked.

Thus, reader, I am myself the matter of my book; you would be unreasonable to spend your leisure on so frivolous and vain a subject.

So farewell. Montaigne, this first day of March, fifteen hundred and eighty.

— reprinted from The Complete Essays of Montaigne, *translated by Donald M. Frame; with the permission of the publisher, Stanford University Press; © 1948, 1957, 1958 by the Board of Trustees of the Leland Stanford Junior University*

Montaigne

On Giving the Lie

Yes, but someone will tell me that this plan of using oneself as a subject to write about would be excusable in rare and famous men who by their reputation had aroused some desire to know them. That is certain; I admit it; and I know full well that to see a man of the common sort, an artisan will hardly raise his eyes from his work, whereas to see a great and prominent personage arrive in a city, men leave workshops and stores empty. It ill befits anyone to make himself known save him who has qualities to be imitated, and whose life and opinions may serve as a model. In the greatness of their deeds Caesar and Xenophon had something to found and establish their narrative upon, as on a just and solid base. Desirable therefore would be the journals of Alexander the Great, and the commentaries that Augustus, Cato, Sulla, Brutus, and others left about their deeds. People love and study the figures of such men, even in bronze and stone.

This remonstrance is very true, but it concerns me only very little:

> Only to friends do I recite, and on request,
> Not to all men, or everywhere. Some will not rest,
> And keep reciting in the Forum or the baths. [HORACE]

I am not building here a statue to erect at the town crossroads, or in a church or a public square:

> I do not aim to swell my page full-blown
> With windy trifles . . . . We two talk alone. [PERSIUS]

This is for a nook in a library, and to amuse a neighbor, a relative, a friend, who may take pleasure in associating and conversing with me again in this image. Others have taken courage to speak of themselves because they found the subject worthy and rich; I, on the contrary, because I have found mine so barren and so meager that no suspicion of ostentation can fall upon my plan.

I willingly judge the actions of others; I give little chance to judge mine because of their nullity. I do not find so much good in myself that I cannot tell it without blushing.

What a satisfaction it would be to me to hear someone tell me, in this way, of the habits, the face, the expression, the favorite remarks, and the fortunes of my ancestors! How attentive I would be! Truly it would spring from a bad nature to be scornful of even the portraits of our friends

— reprinted from The Complete Essays of Montaigne, translated by Donald M. Frame; with the permission of the publisher, Stanford University Press; © 1948, 1957, 1958 by the Board of Trustees of the Leland Stanford Junior University

and predecessors, the form of their clothes and their armor. I keep their handwriting, their seal, the breviary, and a peculiar sword that they used, and I have not banished from my study some long sticks that my father ordinarily carried in his hand. *A father's coat and his ring are the more dear to his children the more they loved him* [SAINT AUGUSTINE].

However, if my descendants have other tastes, I shall have ample means for revenge: for they could not possibly have less concern about me than I shall have about them by that time.

All the contact I have with the public in this book is that I borrow their tools of printing, as being swifter and easier. In recompense, perhaps I shall keep some pat of butter from melting in the market place.

> Lest tunny-fish and olives lack a robe [MARTIAL]
> To mackerel I'll often give a shirt. [CATULLUS]

And if no one reads me, have I wasted my time, entertaining myself for so many idle hours with such useful and agreeable thoughts? In modelling this figure upon myself, I have had to fashion and compose myself so often to bring myself out, that the model itself has to some extent grown firm and taken shape. Painting myself for others, I have painted my inward self with colors clearer than my original ones. I have no more made my book than my book has made me—a book consubstantial with its author, concerned with my own self, an integral part of my life; not concerned with some third-hand, extraneous purpose, like all other books. Have I wasted my time by taking stock of myself so continually, so carefully? For those who go over themselves only in their minds and occasionally in speech do not penetrate to essentials in their examination as does a man who makes that his study, his work, and his trade, who binds himself to keep an enduring account, with all his faith, with all his strength.

Indeed, the most delightful pleasures are digested inwardly, avoid leaving any traces, and avoid the sight not only of the public but of any other person.

How many times has this task diverted me from annoying cogitations! And all frivolous ones should be counted as annoying. Nature has made us a present of a broad capacity for entertaining ourselves apart, and often calls us to do so, to teach us that we owe ourselves in part to society, but in the best part to ourselves. In order to train my fancy even to dream with some order and purpose, and in order to keep it from losing its way and roving with the wind, there is nothing like embodying and registering all the little thoughts that come to it. I listen to my reveries because I have to record them. How many times, irritated by some action that civility and reason kept me from reproving openly, have I disgorged it here, not without ideas of instructing the public! And indeed, these poetic lashes—

> Bang in the eye, bang on the snout,
> Bang on the back of the apish lout! [MAROT]

—imprint themselves even better on paper than on living flesh. What if I lend a slightly more attentive ear to books, since I have been lying in wait to pilfer something from them to adorn or support my own?

I have not studied one bit to make a book; but I have studied a bit because I had made it, if it is studying a bit to skim over and pinch, by his head or his feet, now one author, now another; not at all to form my opinions, but certainly to assist, second, and serve those which I formed long ago.

But whom shall we believe when he talks about himself, in so corrupt an age, seeing that there are few or none whom we can believe when they speak of others, where there is less incentive for lying? The first stage in the corruption of morals is the banishment of truth; for, as Pindar said, to be truthful is the beginning of a great virtue, and is the first article that Plato requires in the governor of his Republic. Our truth of nowadays is not what is, but what others can be convinced of; just as we call "money" not only that which is legal, but also any counterfeit that will pass. Our nation has long been reproached for this vice; for Salvianus of Massilia, who lived in the time of the Emperor Valentinian, says that to the French lying and perjury are not a vice but a manner of speaking. If a man wanted to go this testimony one better, he could say that it is now a virtue to them. Men form and fashion themselves for it as for an honorable practice; for dissimulation is among the most notable qualities of this century.

Thus I have often considered what could be the source of that custom which we observe so religiously, of feeling more bitterly offended when reproached with this vice, which is so common among us, than with any other; and that it should be the worst insult that can be given us in words, to reproach us with lying. On that, I find that it is natural to defend ourselves most for the defects with which we are most besmirched. It seems that in resenting the accusation and growing excited about it, we unburden ourselves to some extent of the guilt; if we have it in fact, at least we condemn it in appearance.

Would it not also be that this reproach seems to involve cowardice and lack of courage? Is there any more obvious cowardice than to deny our own word? Worse yet, to deny what we know?

Lying is an ugly vice, which an ancient paints in most shameful colors when he says that it is giving evidence of contempt for God, and at the same time of fear of men. It is not possible to represent more vividly the horror, the vileness, and the profligacy of it. For what can you imagine uglier than being a coward toward men and bold toward God? Since mutual understanding is brought about solely by way of words, he who breaks his word betrays human society. It is the only instrument by means of which our wills and thoughts communicate, it is the interpreter of our soul. If it fails us, we have no more hold on each other, no more knowledge of each other. If it deceives us, it breaks up all our relations and dissolves all the bonds of our society.

Certain nations of the new Indies (there is no use mentioning their names, which are no more; for the desolation of their conquest—a monstrous and unheard-of case—has extended even to the entire abolition of the names and former knowledge of the places) offered to their gods human blood, but only such as was drawn from their tongue and ears, in expiation of the sin of falsehood, heard as well as uttered.

That worthy fellow from Greece used to say that children play with knucklebones, men with words.

As for the varied etiquette of giving the lie, and our laws of honor in that matter, and the changes they have undergone, I shall put off till another time telling what I know about that, and shall meanwhile learn, if I can, at what time the custom began of weighing and measuring words so exactly, and attaching our honor to them. For it is easy to see that it did not exist in olden times among the Romans and the Greeks. And it has often seemed to me novel and strange to see them giving each other the lie and insulting each other, without having a quarrel over it. The laws of their duty took some other path than ours. Caesar is called now a robber, now a drunkard, to his face. We see how free are the invectives they use against each other, I mean the greatest warlords of both nations, where words are avenged merely by words, and do not lead to other consequences.

The first notable British essayist, Francis Bacon, produced his works of contemplation and reflection while an extremely busy public official. After attending Cambridge University, where he became very interested in science and philosophy, he studied law and then entered Parliament. He was knighted by King James in 1603 and under that monarch received a series of official honors and appointments. In 1618 he became Baron Verulam and Lord Chancellor; three years later he was created Viscount St. Albans. Here his rise stopped; political rivals accused him of corruption and of bribe-taking. He admitted the bribery, but defended his career as a public servant. As a consequence he was deprived of office, fined, and imprisoned. He was, however, soon released, his fine was returned to him, and he retired to the country to devote himself to his studies and writing.

In such books as *The Advancement of Learning* (1605) and *Novum Organum* (1620) Bacon was one of the first advocates of the scientific approach to learning. He insisted that instead of accepting the ideas of so-called "authorities," people should base their conclusions on careful observation and experiment, so that they might learn to control the world of nature.

(1561-1626)

FRANCIS BACON

The *Essays*, from which the following selections are taken, first appeared in 1597; enlarged editions were published in the years 1612 and 1625.

Of Studies

Studies serve for delight, for ornament, and for ability. Their chief use for delight, is in privateness and retiring; for ornament, is in discourse; and for ability, is in the judgment and disposition of business. For expert men can execute, and perhaps judge of particulars, one by one; but the general counsels, and the plots and marshalling of affairs, come best from those that are learned. To spend too much time in studies is sloth; to use them too much for ornament, is affectation; to make judgment wholly by their rules, is the humor of a scholar. They perfect nature, and are perfected by experience: for natural abilities are like natural plants, that need pruning by study; and studies themselves do give forth directions too much at large, except they be bounded in by experience. Crafty men contemn studies, simple men admire them, and wise men use them; for they teach not their own use; but that is a wisdom without them, and above them, won by observation. Read not to contradict and confute; nor to believe and take for granted; nor to find talk and discourse; but to weigh and consider. Some books are to be tasted, others to be swallowed, and some few to be chewed and digested; that is, some books are to be read only in parts; others to be read, but not curiously; and some few to be read wholly, and with diligence and attention. Some books also may be read by deputy, and extracts made of them by others; but that would be only in the less important arguments, and the meaner sort of books; else distilled books are like common distilled waters, flashy things. Reading maketh a full man; conference a ready man; and writing an exact man. And therefore, if a man write little, he had need have a great memory; if he confer little, he had need have a present wit; and if he read little, he had need have much cunning, to seem to know that he doth not. Histories make men wise; poets witty; the mathematics subtile; natural philosophy deep; moral grave; logic and rhetoric able to contend. *Abeunt studia in mores*[1]. Nay there is no stond or impediment in the wit, but may be wrought out by fit studies: like as diseases of the body may have appropriate exercises. Bowling is good for the stone and reins; shooting for the lungs and breast; gentle walking for the stomach; riding for the head; and the like. So if a man's wit be wandering, let him study the mathematics; for in demonstrations, if his wit be called away never so little, he must begin again. If his wit be not apt to distinguish or find differences, let him study the schoolmen; for they are *cymini sectores*[2]. If he be not apt to beat over matters, and to call up one thing to prove and illustrate another, let him study the lawyers' cases. So every defect of the mind may have a special receipt.

— *This and the following selection are reprinted from* Bacon's Essays, *ed. F. G. Selby (English Classics) (London, Macmillan, 1889). For the convenience of the student, paragraphs have been introduced in the selection that follows.*

Of Marriage and Single Life

He that hath wife and children hath given hostages to fortune; for they are impediments to great enterprises, either of virtue or mischief. Certainly the best works, and of greatest merit for the public, have proceeded from the unmarried or childless men; which both in affection and means have married and endowed the public. Yet it were great reason that those that have children should have greatest care of future times; unto which they know they must transmit their dearest pledges.

Some there are, who though they lead a single life, yet their thoughts do end with themselves, and account future times impertinences. Nay, there are some other that account wife and children but as bills of charges. Nay more, there are some foolish rich covetous men, that take a pride in

[1] *Studies pass into the moral being.*
[2] *splitters of cumin seed; i.e. "hair-splitters"*

having no children, because they may be thought so much the richer. For perhaps they have heard some talk, "Such an one is a great rich man," and another except to it, "Yea, but he hath a great charge of children"; as if it were an abatement to his riches. But the most ordinary cause of a single life is liberty, especially in certain self-pleasing and humorous[1] minds, which are so sensible of every restraint, as they will go near to think their girdles and garters to be bonds and shackles.

Unmarried men are best friends, best masters, best servants; but not always best subjects; for they are light to run away; and almost all fugitives are of that condition. A single life doth well with churchmen; for charity will hardly water the ground where it must first fill a pool. It is indifferent for judges and magistrates; for if they be facile and corrupt, you shall have a servant five times worse than a wife. For soldiers, I find the generals commonly in their hortatives put men in mind of their wives and children; and I think the despising of marriage amongst the Turks maketh the vulgar soldier more base.

Certainly wife and children are a kind of discipline of humanity; and single men, though they may be many times more charitable, because their means are less exhaust, yet, on the other side, they are more cruel and hard-hearted (good to make severe inquisitors), because their tenderness is not so oft called upon. Grave natures, led by custom, and therefore constant, are commonly loving husbands; as was said of Ulysses, *vetulam suam prœtulit immortalitati*[2]. Chaste women are often proud and froward, as presuming upon the merit of their chastity. It is one of the best bonds both of chastity and obedience in the wife, if she think her husband wise; which she will never do if she find him jealous.

Wives are young men's mistresses; companions for middle age; and old men's nurses. So as a man may have a quarrel[3] to marry when he will. But yet he was reputed one of the wise men[4], that made answer to the question, when a man should marry—"A young man not yet, an elder man not at all." It is often seen that bad husbands have very good wives; whether it be that it raiseth the price of their husband's kindness when it comes; or that the wives take a pride in their patience. But this never fails, if the bad husbands were of their own choosing, against their friends' consent; for then they will be sure to make good their own folly.

---

[1] *eccentric*

[2] *He preferred his aged wife to immortality.* (*The nymph Calypso had offered to make Ulysses immortal if he would remain with her, but Ulysses refused.*)

[3] *cause or reason*

[4] *Thales of Miletus, the philosopher, was one of the "seven wise men of Greece."*

Today one of the most popular and important poets in the language, John Donne was known in his lifetime chiefly as a prose writer. Born a Catholic, he was educated at Oxford and possibly also at Cambridge. He studied law, travelled on military expeditions to Europe, and for some time hoped for a career in the public service. In 1615 he became an Anglican priest and eventually Dean of St. Paul's Cathedral. It was here that his sermons established for him his reputation as a prose stylist. His earliest biographer, Izaak Walton, said of him that he preached "like an Angel from a cloud, but in none." The "Meditation" from <u>Devotions Upon Emergent Occasions</u>

(1573-1631)

JOHN DONNE

(1624), which appears here, was written after Donne had recovered from a lengthy and near-fatal illness, the "emergent occasion" which is referred to in the title of the work.

Meditation

Nunc Lento Sonitu Dicunt, Morieris.

(Now, this bell tolling softly for another, says to me: Thou must die.)

Perchance he for whom this bell tolls, may be so ill, as that he knows not it tolls for him; and perchance I may think myself so much better than I am, as that they who are about me, and see my state, may have caused it to toll for me, and I know not that. The church is Catholic, universal, so are all her actions; all that she does, belongs to all. When she baptizes a child, that action concerns me; for that child is thereby connected to that head which is my head too, and ingrafted into that body, whereof I am a member. And when she buries a man, that action concerns me: all mankind is of one author, and is one volume; when one man dies, one chapter is not torn out of the book, but translated into a better language; and every chapter must be so translated; God employs several translators; some pieces are translated by age, some by sickness, some by war, some by justice; but God's hand is in every translation, and his hand shall bind up all our scattered leaves again for that library where every book shall lie open to one another. As therefore the bell that rings to a sermon calls not upon the preacher only, but upon the congregation to come; so this bell calls us all: but how much more me, who am brought so near the door by this sickness. There was a contention as far as a suit (in which both piety and dignity, religion and estimation, were mingled), which of the religious orders should ring to prayers first in the morning; and it was determined, that they should ring first that rose earliest. If we understand aright the dignity of this bell that tolls for our evening prayer, we would be glad to make it ours, by rising

9

early in that application, that it might be ours, as well as his, whose indeed it is. The bell doth toll for him that thinks it doth; and though it intermit again, yet from that minute that that occasion wrought upon him, he is united to God. Who casts not up his eye to the sun when it rises? but who takes off his eye from a comet when that breaks out? Who bends not his ear to any bell, which upon any occasion rings? but who can remove it from that bell, which is passing a piece of himself out of this world? No man is an island, entire of itself; every man is a piece of the continent, a part of the main; if a clod be washed away by the sea, Europe is the less, as well as if a promontory were, as well as if a manor of thy friend's or of thine own were; any man's death diminishes me, because I am involved in mankind; and therefore never send to know for whom the bell tolls; it tolls for thee. Neither can we call this a begging of misery or a borrowing of misery, as though we were not miserable enough of ourselves, but must fetch in more from the next house, in taking upon us the misery of our neighbors. Truly it were an excusable covetousness if we did; for affliction is a treasure, and scarce any man hath enough of it. No man hath affliction enough that is not matured, and ripened by it, and made fit for God by that affliction. If a man carry treasure in bullion, or in a wedge of gold, and have none coined into current money, his treasure will not defray him as he travels. Tribulation is treasure in the nature of it, but it is not current money in the use of it, except we get nearer and nearer our home, heaven, by it. Another man may be sick too, and sick to death, and this affliction may lie in his bowels, as gold in a mine, and be of no use to him; but this bell, that tells me of his affliction, digs out, and applies that gold to me; if by this consideration of another's danger, I take mine own into contemplation, and so secure myself, by making my recourse to my God, who is our only security.

— *reprinted from* The Complete Poetry and Selected Prose of John Donne, *ed. Chas. M. Coffin (New York, Random House, Inc., 1952)*

Following his education at the Charterhouse School and Oxford University, Richard Steele entered the army (1694) and achieved the rank of "Captain" for his service under the Duke of Ormond. His first publication was The Christian Hero *(1701) and this treatise, which revealed his ideas of reform, was followed by several plays which enjoyed some measure of success and popularity. Steele became interested in politics in 1707 when he was appointed "gazetteer," and later became a member of Parliament (1713). He was knighted by George I (1715) in spite of his expulsion from Parliament over a controversial publication. Steele is important in the history of English literature as a writer of the periodical essay. With Joseph Addision, he wrote* The Tatler *(1709-1711) and* The Spectator *(1711-1712): both newspapers were characterized by good-natured humor and clever satire. He also founded and was the chief contributor to two other periodical journals of note,* The Guardian *and* The Englishman. *His involvement in politics, however, eventually*

(1672-1729)

RICHARD STEELE

caused him to lose much of his prestige and led to an estrangement from Addison. He left London in 1724.

Prospectus

<u>*The Tatler*</u>, *No. 1*   *Tuesday, April 12, 1709*

Though the other papers, which are published for the use of the good people of England, have certainly very wholesome effects, and are laudable in their particular kinds, they do not seem to come up to the main design of such narrations, which, I humbly presume, should be principally intended for the use of politic persons, who are so public-spirited as to neglect their own affairs, to look into transactions of state. Now these gentlemen, for the most part being persons of strong zeal and weak intellects, it is both a charitable and necessary work to offer something, whereby such worthy and well-affected members of the commonwealth may be instructed, after their reading, what to think: which shall be the end and purpose of this my paper, wherein I shall, from time to time, report and consider all matters of what kind soever that shall occur to me, and publish such my advices and reflections every Tuesday, Thursday, and Saturday, in the week, for the convenience of the post.

I resolve also to have something which may be of entertainment to the fair sex, in honor of whom I have invented the title of this Paper. I therefore earnestly desire all persons, without distinction, to take it in for the present *gratis*, and hereafter at the price of one penny, forbidding all hawkers to take more for it at their peril. And I desire all persons to consider, that I am at a very great charge for proper materials for this work, as well as that, before I resolved upon it, I had settled a correspondence in all parts of the known and knowing world. And forasmuch as this globe is not trodden upon by mere drudges of business only, but that men of spirit and genius are justly to be esteemed as considerable agents in it, we shall not, upon a dearth of news, present you with musty foreign edicts, and dull proclamations, but shall divide our relation of the passages which occur in action or discourse throughout this town, as well as elsewhere, under such dates of places as may prepare you for the matter you are to expect in the following manner.

All accounts of gallantry, pleasure, and entertainment, shall be under the article of White's *Chocolate-house;* poetry, under that of Will's *Coffee-house;* learning, under the title of *Grecian;* foreign and domestic news, you will have from Saint James's *Coffee-house;* and what else I have to offer on any other subject shall be dated from *my own Apartment.*

I once more desire my reader to consider, that as I cannot keep an ingenious man to go daily to Will's under two-pence each day, merely for his charges; to White's under six-pence; nor to the Grecian, without allowing him some plain Spanish, to be as able as others at the learned table; and that a good observer cannot speak with even Kidney at Saint James's without clean linen; I say, these considerations will, I hope, make all persons willing to comply with my humble request (when my *gratis* stock is exhausted) of a penny apiece; especially since they are sure of some proper amusement, and that it is impossible for me to want means to entertain them, having, besides the force of my own parts, the power of divination, and that I can, by casting a figure, tell you all that will happen before it comes to pass.

But this last faculty I shall use very sparingly, and speak but of few things until they are passed, for fear of divulging matters which may offend our superiors.

— *this and the following selection reprinted from* The Tatler, or Lucubrations of Isaac Bickerstaff, Esq. *(London, 1772); titles are not in the original*

The Editor's Troubles

The Tatler, *No. 164*   *Thursday, April 27, 1710*

I have lately been looking over the many packets of letters which I have received from all quarters of Great-Britain, as well as from foreign countries, since my entering upon the office of Censor; and indeed am very much surprised to see so great a number of them, and pleased to think that I have so far increased the revenue of the post-office. As this collection will grow daily, I have digested it into several bundles, and made proper indorsements on each particular letter; it being my design, when I lay down the work that I am now engaged in, to erect a paper office, and give it to the public.

I could not but make several observations upon reading over the letters of my correspondents: As first of all, on the different tastes that reign in the different parts of this city. I find, by the approbations which are given me, that I am seldom famous on the same days on both sides of Temple-bar; and that when I am in the greatest repute within the liberties, I dwindle at the court end of the town. Sometimes I sink in both these places at the same time; but for my comfort, my name hath then been up in the districts of Wapping and Rotherhithe. Some of my correspondents desire me to be always serious, and others to be always merry. Some of them entreat me to go to bed and fall into a dream, and like me better when I am asleep than when I am awake: others advise me to sit all night upon the stars, and be more frequent in my astrological observations; for that a vision is not properly a Lucubration. Some of my readers thank me for filling my Paper with the flowers of antiquity, others desire news from Flanders. Some approve my criticisms on the dead, and others my censures on the living. For this reason I once resolved, in the new edition of my works, to range my several Papers under distinct heads, according as their principal design was to benefit and instruct the different capacities of my readers; and to follow the example of some very great authors, by writing at the head of each discourse, *Ad Aulam, Ad Academiam, Ad Populum, Ad Clerum.*

There is no particular in which my correspondents of all ages, conditions, sexes, and complexions, universally agree, except only in their thirst after scandal. It is impossible to conceive, how many have recommended their neighbours to me upon this account, or how unmercifully I have been abused by several unknown hands, for not publishing the secret histories of cuckoldom that I have received from almost every street in town.

It would indeed be very dangerous for me to read over the many praises and eulogiums, which come post to me from all corners of the nation, were they not mixed with many checks, reprimands, scurrilities, and reproaches; which several of my good-natured countrymen cannot forbear sending me, though it often costs them two-pence or a groat before they can convey them to my hands: so that sometimes when I am put into the best humour in the world, after having read a panegyric upon my performances, and looked upon myself as a benefactor to the British nation, the next letter, perhaps, I open, begins with "You old doting scoundrel!—Are not you a sad dog?—Sirrah, you deserve to have your nose slit"; and the like ingenious conceits. These little mortifications are necessary to suppress that pride and vanity which naturally arise in the mind of a received author, and enable me to bear the reputation which my courteous readers bestow upon me, without becoming a coxcomb by it. It was for the same reason, that when a Roman general entered the city in the pomp of triumph, the commonwealth allowed of several little drawbacks to his reputation, by conniving at such of the rabble as repeated libels and lampoons upon him within his hearing; and by that means engaged his thoughts upon his weakness and imperfections, as well as on the merits that advanced him to so great honours. The conqueror, however, was not the less esteemed for being a man in some particulars, because he appeared as a god in others.

There is another circumstance in which my countrymen have dealt very perversely with me; and that is, in searching not only into my life, but also into the lives of my ancestors. If there has been a blot in my family for these ten generations, it hath been discovered by some or other of my correspondents. In short, I find the ancient family of the Bickerstaffs has suffered very much through the malice and prejudice of my enemies. Some of them twit me in the teeth with the conduct of my aunt Margery: Nay, there are some who have been so disingenuous, as to throw Maud the milkmaid into my dish, notwithstanding I myself was the first who discovered that alliance. I reap, however, many benefits from the malice of these enemies, as they let me see my own faults, and give me a view of myself in the worst light; as they hinder me from being blown up by flattery and self-conceit; as they make me keep a watchful eye over my own actions; and at the same time make me cautious how I talk of others, and particularly of my friends or relations, or value myself upon the antiquity of my family.

But the most formidable part of my correspondents are those, whose letters are filled with threats and menaces. I have been treated so often after this manner, that, not thinking it sufficient to fence well, in which I am now arrived at the utmost perfection, and to carry pistols about me, which I have always tucked within my girdle; I several months since made my will, settled my estate, and took leave of my friends, looking upon myself as no better than a dead man. Nay, I went so far as to write a long letter to the most intimate acquaintance I have in the world, under the character of a departed person; giving him an account of what brought me to that untimely end, and of the fortitude with which I met it. This letter being too long for the present paper, I intend to print it by itself very suddenly; and at the same time I must confess, I took my hint of it from the behaviour of an old soldier in the civil wars, who was corporal of a company in a regiment of foot, about the same time that I myself was a cadet in the King's army.

This gentleman was taken by the enemy; and the two parties were upon such terms at that time that we did not treat each other as prisoners of war, but as traitors and rebels. The poor corporal, being condemned to die, wrote a letter to his wife when under sentence of execution. He writ on the Thursday, and was to be executed on the Friday; but, considering that the letter would not come to his wife's hands, until Saturday, the day after execution, and being at that time more scrupulous than ordinary in speaking exact truth, he formed his letter rather according to the posture of his affairs when she should read it, than as they stood when he sent it: though it must be confessed, there is a certain perplexity in the style of it, which the reader will easily pardon, considering his circumstances.

"Dear Wife,

"Hoping you are in good health, as I am at this present writing; this is to let you know, that yesterday, between the hours of eleven and twelve, I was *hanged, drawn,* and *quartered.* I died very penitently, and everybody thought my case very hard. Remember me kindly to my poor fatherless children.

Yours, until death,

W.B."

It so happened, that this honest fellow was relieved by a party of his friends, and had the satisfaction to see all the rebels hanged who had been his enemies. I must not omit a circumstance which exposed him to raillery his whole life after. Before the arrival of the next post, that would have set all things clear, his wife was married to a second husband, who lived in the peaceable possession of her; and the corporal, who was a man of plain understanding, did not care to stir in the matter, as knowing that she had the news of his death under his own hand, which she might have produced upon that occasion.

A Prize Fight

Being a Person of insatiable Curiosity, I could not forbear going on *Wednesday* last to a Place of no small Renown for the Gallantry of the lower Order of *Britons,* namely, to the Bear-Garden at *Hockley in the Hole;* where (as a whitish brown Paper, put into my Hands in the Street, inform'd me) there was to be a Tryal of Skill to be exhibited between Two Masters of the Noble Science of Defence, at Two of the Clock precisely. I was not a little charm'd with the Solemnity of the Challenge, which ran thus:

I James Miller, *Serjeant, (lately come from the Frontiers of* Portugal) *Master of the Noble Science of Defence, hearing in most Places where I have been of the great Fame of* Timothy Buck *of* London, *Master of the said Science, do invite him to meet me, and exercise at the several Weapons following, viz.*

15

Back-Sword,	Single Falchon,
Sword and Dagger,	Case of Falchons,
Sword and Buckler,	Quarter-Staff.

If the generous Ardour in *James Miller* to dispute the Reputation of *Timothy Buck*, had something resembling the old Heroes of Romance, *Timothy Buck* return'd Answer in the same Paper with the like Spirit, adding a little Indignation at being challenged, and seeming to condescend to fight *James Miller*, not in regard to *Miller* himself, but in that, as the Fame went out, he had fought *Parks* of *Coventry*. The Acceptance of the Combat ran in these words:

I Timothy Buck, *of* Clare-Market, *Master of the Noble Science of Defence, hearing he did fight Mr.* Parks *of* Coventry, *will not fail (God willing) to meet this fair Inviter at the Time and Place appointed desiring a clear Stage and no Favour.*

Vivat Regina.

I shall not here look back on the Spectacles of the *Greeks* and *Romans* of this Kind, but must believe this Custom took its Rise from the Ages of Knight-Errantry; from those who lov'd one Woman so well, that they hated all Men and Women else; from those who would fight you, whether you were or were not of their Mind; from those who demanded the Combat of their Contemporaries; both for admiring their Mistress or discommending her. I cannot therefore but lament, that the terrible Part of the ancient Fight is preserv'd, when the amorous Side of it is forgotten. We have retain'd the Barbarity, but lost the Gallantry of the old Combatants. I could wish, methinks, these Gentlemen had consulted me in the Promulgation of the conflict. I was obliged by a fair young Maid, whom I understood to be called *Elizabeth Preston*, Daughter of the Keeper of the Garden, with a Glass of Water; whom I imagined might have been, for Form's sake, the general Representative of the Lady fought for, and from her Beauty the proper *Amarillis* on these Occasions. It wou'd have ran better in the Challenge: *I* James Miller, *Serjeant, who have travell'd Parts abroad, and came last from the Frontiers of* Portugal, *for the love of* Elizabeth Preston, *do assert, That the said* Elizabeth *is the Fairest of Women.* Then the Answer: *I* Timothy Buck, *who have stay'd in* Great Britain *during all the War in Foreign Parts, for the sake of* Susanna Page, *do deny that* Elizabeth Preston *is so fair as the said* Susanna Page. Let *Susanna Page* look on, and I desire of *James Miller* no Favour.

This would give the Battle quite another Turn; and a proper Station for the Ladies, whose Complexion was disputed by the Sword, would animate the Disputants with a more gallant Incentive than the Expectation of Money from the Spectators; tho' I would not have that neglected, but thrown to that Fair One, whose Lover was approved by the Donor.

Yet, considering the Thing wants such Amendments, it was carry'd with great Order. *James Miller* came on first, preceded by two disabled Drummers, to shew, I suppose, that the Prospect of maimed Bodies did not in the least deter him. There ascended with the daring *Miller* a Gentleman, whose Name I could not learn, with a dogged Air, as unsatisfy'd that he was not Principal. This Son of Anger lower'd at the whole Assembly, and weighing himself as he march'd around from Side to Side, with a stiff Knee and Shoulder, he gave Intimations of the Purpose he smother'd till he saw the Issue of this Encounter. *Miller* had a blue Ribband ty'd round in the Sword-Arm; which Ornament I conceive to be the Remain of that Custom of wearing a Mistress's Favour on such Occasions of old.

Miller is a Man of six Foot eight Inches Height, of a kind but bold Aspect, well-fashion'd, and ready of his Limbs; and such a Readiness as spoke his Ease in them, was obtain'd from a Habit of Motion in Military Exercise.

The Expectation of the Spectators was now almost at its Height, and the Crowd pressing in, several active Persons thought they were placed rather according to their Fortune than their Merit, and took it in their Heads to prefer themselves from the open Area, or Pit, to the Galleries. This dispute between Desert and Property brought many to the Ground, and raised others in proportion to the highest Seats by Turns for the Space of ten Minutes, till *Timothy Buck* came on, the whole Assembly giving up their Disputes, turn'd their Eyes upon the Champions. Then it was that every Man's Affection turned to one or the other irresistibly. A judicious Gentleman near me said, *I could, methinks, be* Miller's *Second, but I had rather have* Buck *for mine*. *Miller* had an audacious Look that took the Eye; *Buck* a perfect Composure, that engaged the Judgement. *Buck* came on in a plain Coat, and kept all his Air till the Instant of Engaging; at which Time he undress'd to his Shirt, his Arm adorned with a Bandage of red Ribband. No one can describe the sudden Concern in the whole Assembly; the most tumultuous Crowd in Nature was as still and as much engaged, as if all their Lives depended on the first Blow. The Combatants met in the Middle of the Stage, and shaking Hands as removing all Malice, they retired with much Grace to the Extremities of it; from whence they immediately faced about, and approached each other, *Miller* with an Heart full of Resolution, *Buck* with a watchful untroubled Countenance; *Buck* regarding principally his own Defence, *Miller* chiefly thoughtful of annoying his Opponent. It is not easy to describe the many Escapes and imperceptible Defences between two Men of quick Eyes and ready Limbs; but *Miller's* Heat laid him open to the Rebuke of the calm *Buck*, by a large Cut on the Forehead. Much Effusion of Blood covered his Eyes in a Moment, and the Huzzas of the Crowd undoubtedly quickened the Anguish. The Assembly was divided into Parties upon their different ways of Fighting; while a poor Nymph in one of the Galleries apparently suffered for *Miller*, and burst into a Flood of

Tears. As soon as his Wound was wrapped up, he came on again with a little Rage, which still disabled him further. But what brave Man can be wounded into more Patience and Caution? The next was a warm eager Onset, which ended in a decisive Stroke on the left Leg of *Miller*. The Lady in the Gallery, during this second Strife, covered her Face; and for my Part, I could not keep my Thoughts from being mostly employed on the Consideration of her unhappy Circumstance that Moment, hearing the Clash of Swords, and apprehending Life or Victory concerned her Lover in every Blow, but not daring to satisfy her self on whom they fell. The Wound was exposed to the View of all who could delight in it, and sewed up on the Stage. The surly Second of *Miller* declared at this Time, that he would that Day Fortnight fight Mr. *Buck* at the same Weapons, declaring himself the Master of the renowned *Gorman;* but *Buck* denied him the Honour of that courageous Disciple, and asserting that he himself had taught that Champion, accepted the Challenge.

There is something in Nature very unaccountable on such Occasions, when we see the People take a certain painful Gratification in beholding these Encounters. Is it Cruelty that administers this Sort of Delight? or is it a Pleasure which is taken in the Exercise of Pity? It was methought pretty remarkable, that the Business of the Day being a Tryal of Skill, the Popularity did not run so high as one would have expected on the Side of *Buck*. Is it that People's Passions have their Rise in Self-Love, and thought themselves (in Spite of all the Courage they had) liable to the Fate of *Miller* but could not so easily think themselves qualified like *Buck?*

Tully speaks of this Custom with less Horrour than one would expect, tho' he confesses it was much abused in his Time, and seems directly to approve of it under its first Regulations, when Criminals only fought before the People. *Crudele Gladiatorum spectaculum & inhumanum nonnullis videri solet; & haud scio annon ita sit ut nunc fit; com vero sontes ferro depugnabant, auribus fortasse multa, oculis quidem nulla, poterat esse fortior contra dolorem & mortem disciplina.* The Shows of Gladiators may be thought barbarous and inhumane, and I know not but it is so as it is now practised; but in those Times when only Criminals were Combatants, the Ear perhaps might receive many better Instructions, but it is impossible that any thing which affects our Eyes, should fortify us so well against Pain and Death.

— *This selection is reprinted from* The Spectator, *Vol. IV, ed. D. F. Bond (Oxford, Clarendon Press, 1965); with permission of the publisher. The editors have attempted to retain the flavor of the original in spelling and punctuation; the title is not in the original.*

Joseph Addison was educated at the Charterhouse School and later at Queen's College, Oxford, where he was an outstanding classics student. He received a Master of Arts degree in 1693 and after travelling extensively on the continent, published two books, The Campaign and Remarks on Several Parts of Italy; which launched his literary career. Like Richard Steele, he was keenly interested in politics, and was appointed Under-Secretary of State in 1706; he became a Whig member of Parliament in 1708.

Addison collaborated with Steele first on The Tatler (1709-1711), and later on The Spectator (1711-1712) — to which he contributed the majority of essays. His most famous essays from The Spectator are those of literary criticism and those written about the fictitious Sir Roger de Coverley. In 1713, Addison's tragedy, Cato, was produced with success, and was followed by a prose comedy, The Drummer, which was a failure. From 1715 to 1716 he wrote a political newspaper, The Freeholder, and in 1717, after his marriage to the Countess of Warwick, he was appointed Secretary of State. He retired from public office in 1718.

(1672-1719)

JOSEPH ADDISON

The Head-dress

There is not so variable a thing in Nature as a Lady's Head-dress: Within my own Memory I have known it rise and fall above thirty Degrees. About ten Years ago it shot up to a very great Height, insomuch that the Female Part of our Species were much taller than the Men. The Women were of such an enormous Stature, that *we appeared as grasshoppers before them:* At present the whole Sex is in a Manner dwarfed and shrunk into a Race of Beauties that seems almost another Species. I remember several Ladies, who were once very near seven Foot high, that at present want some Inches of five: How they came to be thus curtailed I cannot learn; whether the whole Sex be at present under any Penance which we know nothing of, or whether they have cast their Head-dresses in order to surprize us with something in that Kind which shall be entirely new; or whether some of the tallest of the Sex, being too cunning for the rest, have contrived this Method to make themselves appear sizeable, is still a Secret; tho' I find most are of Opinion, they are at present like Trees new lopped and pruned, that will certainly sprout up and flourish with greater heads than before. For my own Part, as I do not love to be insulted by Women who are taller than my self, I admire the Sex much more in their present Humiliation, which has reduced them to their natural Dimensions, than when they had extended their Persons, and lengthened themselves out into formidable and gigantick figures. I am not for adding to the beautiful Edifices of Nature, nor for raising any whimsical Superstructure upon her Plans: I must therefore repeat it, that I am highly pleased with the Coiffure now in Fashion; and think it shews the good Sense which at present very much reigns among the valuable Part of the Sex. One may observe, that Women in all Ages have taken more Pains than Men to adorn the Outside of their Heads; and indeed I very much admire, that those Female Architects who raise such wonderful structures out of Ribbands, Lace and Wire, have not been recorded for their respective Inventions. It is certain there have been as many Orders in these Kinds of Building, as in those which have been made of Marble: Sometimes they rise in the Shape of a Pyramid, sometimes like a Tower, and sometimes like a Steeple.[1]

The Fan Exercise

I do not know whether to call the following letter a satire upon coquettes, or a representation of their several fantastical accomplishments, or what other title to give it; but as it is I shall communicate it to the public. It will sufficiently explain its own intentions, so that I shall give it my reader at length, without either preface or postscript.

MR. SPECTATOR,

Women are armed with fans as men with swords, and sometimes do more execution with them. To the end, therefore, that ladies may be entire mistresses of the weapon which they bear, I have erected an academy for the training up of young women in the *Exercise of the Fan*, according to the most fashionable airs and motions that are now practised at court. The ladies who carry fans under me are drawn up twice a day in my great hall, where they are instructed in the use of their arms, and exercised by the following words of command:

> *Handle your Fans,*
> *Unfurl your Fans,*
> *Discharge your Fans,*
> *Ground your Fans,*
> *Recover your Fans,*
> *Flutter your Fans.*

By the right observation of these few plain words of command, a woman of

[1] *To illustrate the usage of the time, "The Head-dress" is printed much as it appeared in the original edition. "The Fan Exercise," "The Petticoat,"and "Sir Roger at Church" have been revised to conform more to present practice; the titles are not in the original.*

a tolerable genius who will apply herself diligently to her exercise for the space of but one half year, shall be able to give her fan all the graces that can possibly enter into that little modish machine.

But to the end that my readers may form to themselves a right notion of this exercise, I beg leave to explain it to them in all its parts. When my female regiment is drawn up in array, with every one her weapon in her hand, upon my giving the word to *Handle their Fans*, each of them shakes her fan at me with a smile, then gives her right-hand woman a tap upon the shoulder, then presses her lips with the extremity of her fan, then lets her arms fall in an easy motion, and stands in readiness to receive the next word of command. All this is done with a closed fan, and is generally learned in the first week.

The next motion is that of *Unfurling the Fan*, in which are comprehended several little flirts and vibrations, as also gradual and deliberate openings, with many voluntary fallings asunder in the fan itself, that are seldom learned under a month's practice. This part of the exercise pleases the spectators more than any other, as it discovers on a sudden an infinite number of cupids, garlands, altars, birds, beasts, rainbows, and the like agreeable figures, that display themselves to view, whilst everyone in the regiment holds a picture in her hand.

Upon my giving the word to *Discharge their Fans*, they give one general crack, that may be heard at a considerable distance when the wind sits fair. This is one of the most difficult parts of the exercise, but I have several ladies with me, who at their first entrance could not give a pop loud enough to be heard at the further end of a room, who can now discharge a fan in such a manner that it shall make a report like a pocket pistol. I have likewise taken care (in order to hinder young women from letting off their fans in wrong places or unsuitable occasions) to show upon what subject the crack of a fan may come in properly. I have likewise invented a fan with which a girl of sixteen, by the help of a little wind which is enclosed about one of the largest sticks, can make as loud a crack as a woman of fifty with an ordinary fan.

When the fans are thus discharged, the word of command in course is to *Ground their Fans*. This teaches a lady to quit her fan gracefully when she throws it aside in order to take up a pack of cards, adjust a curl of hair, replace a fallen pin, or apply herself to any other matter of importance. This part of the exercise, as it only consists in tossing a fan with an air upon a long table (which stands by for that purpose) may be learned in two days' time as well as in a twelvemonth.

When my female regiment is thus disarmed, I generally let them walk about the room for some time; when on a sudden (like ladies that look upon their watches after a long visit) they all of them hasten to their arms, catch them up in a hurry, and place themselves in their proper stations upon my calling out *Recover your Fans*. This part of the exercise is not difficult, provided a woman applies her thoughts to it.

The *Fluttering of the Fan* is the last, and, indeed, the masterpiece of the whole exercise; but if a lady does not misspend her time, she may make herself mistress of it in three months. I generally lay aside the dog-days and the hot time of the summer for the teaching of this part of the exercise; for as soon as ever I pronounce *Flutter your Fans*, the place is filled with so many zephyrs and gentle breezes as are very refreshing in that season of the year, though they might be dangerous to ladies of a tender constitution in any other.

There is an infinite variety of motions to be made use of in the flutter of a fan: there is the angry flutter, the modest flutter, the timorous flutter, the confused flutter, the merry flutter, and the amorous flutter. Not to be tedious, there is scarce any emotion in the mind which does not produce a suitable agitation in the fan; insomuch, that if I only see the fan of a disciplined lady, I know very well whether she laughs, frowns, or blushes. I have seen a fan so very angry, that it would have been dangerous for the absent lover who provoked it to have come within the wind of it; and at other times so very languishing, that I have been glad for the lady's sake the lover was at a sufficient distance from it. I need not add that a fan is either a prude or coquette, according to the nature of the person who bears it. To conclude my letter, I must acquaint you that I have from my own observations compiled a little treatise for the use of my scholars, entitled *The Passions of the Fan*, which I will communicate to you, if you think it may be of use to the public. I shall have a general review on Thursday next, to which you shall be very welcome if you will honor it with your presence.

I am, &c.

P.S. I teach young gentlemen the whole art of gallanting a fan.
N.B. I have several little plain fans made for this use, to avoid expense.

The Petticoat

. . . the fair sex are run into great extravagancies. Their petticoats, which began to heave and swell before you left us, are now blown up into a most enormous concave, and rise every day more and more. In short, Sir, since our women know themselves to be out of the eye of the SPECTATOR, they will be kept within no compass. You praised them a little too soon for the modesty of their head-dresses. For as the humor of a sick person is often driven out of one limb into another, their superfluity of ornaments, instead of being entirely banished, seems only fallen from their heads upon their lower parts. What they have lost in height they make up in breadth, and contrary to all rules of architecture widen the foundations at the same time that they shorten the superstructure . . . .

Should this fashion get among the ordinary people, our public ways would be so crowded that we should want street-room. Several congregations of the best fashion find themselves already very much straitened, and, if the mode increases, I wish it may not drive many ordinary women into meetings and conventicles.[1] Should our sex at the same time take it into their heads to wear trunk-breeches[2] (as who knows what their indignation at this female treatment may drive them to) a man and his wife would fill a whole pew.

When I survey this new-fashioned rotonda in all its parts, I cannot but think of the old philosopher, who after having entered into an Egyptian temple, and looked about for the idol of the place, at length discovered a little black monkey enshrined in the midst of it, upon which he could not forbear crying out (to the great scandal of the worshippers), "What a magnificent palace is here for such a ridiculous inhabitant!"

Sir Roger at Church

I am always very well pleased with a country Sunday, and think, if keeping holy the seventh day were only a human institution, it would be the best method that could have been thought of for the polishing and civilizing of mankind. It is certain the country people would soon degenerate into a kind of savages and barbarians, were there not such frequent returns of a stated time in which the whole village meet together with their best faces, and in their cleanliest habits, to converse with one another upon indifferent subjects, hear their duties explained to them, and join together in adoration of the Supreme Being. Sunday clears away the rust of the whole week, not only as it refreshes in their minds the notions of religion, but as it puts both the sexes upon appearing in their most agreeable forms, and exerting all such qualities as are apt to give them a figure in the eye of the village. A country fellow distinguishes himself as much in the church-

---

[1] *The ironical suggestion is that many women will find themselves crowded out of the Established Church, where the fashion prevails, and will join the Dissenters.*
[2] *full bag-like breeches covering the hips and upper thighs, sometimes stuffed*

yard as a citizen does upon the Change[1], the whole parish politics being generally discussed in that place either after sermon or before the bell rings.

My friend Sir Roger, being a good churchman, has beautified the inside of his church with several texts of his own choosing; he has likewise given a handsome pulpit cloth, and railed in the communion table at his own expense. He has often told me that at his coming to his estate he found his parishioners very irregular; and that in order to make them kneel and join in the responses, he gave every one of them a hassock and a Common Prayer Book; and at the same time employed an itinerant singing master, who goes about the country for that purpose, to instruct them rightly in the tunes of the psalms, upon which they now very much value themselves, and indeed outdo most of the country churches that I have ever heard.

As Sir Roger is landlord to the whole congregation, he keeps them in very good order, and will suffer nobody to sleep in it besides himself; for if by chance he has been surprised into a short nap at sermon, upon recovering out of it he stands up and looks about him, and if he sees anybody else nodding, either wakes them himself, or sends his servant to them. Several other of the old knight's particularities break out upon these occasions: sometimes he will be lengthening out a verse in the singing psalms half a minute after the rest of the congregation have done with it; sometimes, when he is pleased with the matter of his devotion, he pronounces *Amen* three or four times to the same prayer; and sometimes stands up when everybody else is upon their knees, to count the congregation, or see if any of his tenants are missing.

I was yesterday very much surprised to hear my old friend, in the midst of the service, calling out to one John Matthews to mind what he was about, and not disturb the congregation. This John Matthews, it seems, is remarkable for being an idle fellow, and at that time was kicking his heels for his diversion. This authority of the knight, though exerted in that odd manner which accompanies him in all circumstances of life, has a very good effect upon the parish, who are not polite enough to see anything ridiculous in his behavior; besides that, the general good sense and worthiness of his character make his friends observe these little singularities as foils that rather set off than blemish his good qualities.

As soon as the sermon is finished, nobody presumes to stir till Sir Roger is gone out of the church. The knight walks down from his seat in the chancel, between a double row of his tenants that stand bowing to him on each side, and every now and then he inquires how such an one's wife, or mother, or son, or father do, whom he does not see at church, which is understood as a secret reprimand to the person that is absent.

The chaplain has often told me, that upon a catechizing day, when Sir

---

1 *exchange; place where merchants, brokers, and bankers meet to transact business*

Roger has been pleased with a boy that answers well, he has ordered a Bible to be given him next day for his encouragement, and sometimes accompanies it with a flitch of bacon to his mother. Sir Roger has likewise added five pounds a year to the clerk's place, and that he may encourage the young fellows to make themselves perfect in the church service, has promised upon the death of the present incumbent, who is very old, to bestow it according to merit.

The fair understanding between Sir Roger and his chaplain, and their mutual concurrence in doing good, is the more remarkable because the very next village is famous for the differences and contentions that rise between the parson and the squire, who live in a perpetual state of war. The parson is always preaching at the squire, and the squire, to be revenged on the parson, never comes to church. The squire has made all his tenants atheists and tithe-stealers; while the parson instructs them every Sunday in the dignity of his order, and insinuates to them, in almost every sermon, that he is a better man than his patron. In short, matters are come to such an extremity that the squire has not said his prayers either in public or private this half year, and that the parson threatens him, if he does not mend his manners, to pray for him in the face of the whole congregation.

Feuds of this nature, though too frequent in the country, are very fatal to the ordinary people, who are so used to be dazzled with riches that they pay as much deference to the understanding of a man of an estate as of a man of learning, and are very hardly brought to regard any truth, how important soever it may be, that is preached to them, when they know there are several men of five hundred a year who do not believe it.

— selections by Addison reprinted, with some alterations, from The Spectator, Vols. I and II, ed. D. F. Bond (Oxford, Clarendon Press, 1965); with permission of the publisher

Samuel Johnson, the son of a Lichfield bookseller, spent much of his youth reading difficult books and, upon entering Oxford in 1728, acquired a reputation as the best-qualified student the university had ever had. Because of his poverty, however, he was unable to complete a degree, and he therefore left the university for employment, first as an usher at Market Bosworth school and later as the headmaster of his own school at Edial. In 1737, Johnson closed his school and with his wife and a student, David Garrick, set out for London, where he was destined to become the most influential literary figure of the century.

In London, Johnson was a regular contributor to The Gentleman's Magazine and published a number of individual works, including London (1738), The Life of Savage (1744), and The Vanity of Human Wishes (1749). He also published several series of periodical essays—The Rambler and The Idler, and a didactic romance entitled Rasselas (1759). His famous two-volume Dictionary, which required more than fifteen years to complete, was published in 1755.

Dr. Johnson's other major works included his well-known account of a journey to Scotland with Boswell (A Journey to the Western Isles of Scotland), an eight-volume edition of Shakespeare, and a ten-volume critical and biographical work entitled Lives of the Poets.

Dr. Johnson became well known for his love of argument and lively conversation and many of his quips and sayings have been recorded by James Boswell in his Life of Johnson. Of Johnson's appearance at their first meeting, Boswell writes: "His brown suit of clothes looked very rusty; he had on a little old shrivelled unpowdered wig, which was too small for his head; his shirt neck and the knees of his breeches were loose; his black worsted stockings ill drawn up; and he had a pair of unbuckled shoes by way of slippers. But all these slovenly particularities were forgotten the moment he began to talk."

(1709-1784)

SAMUEL JOHNSON

The Uncertainty of Friendship

The Idler, No. 23   *Saturday, September 23, 1758*

Life has no pleasure higher or nobler than that of friendship. It is painful to consider that this sublime enjoyment may be impaired or destroyed by innumerable causes, and that there is no human possession of which the duration is less certain.

Many have talked, in very exalted language, of the perpetuity of friendship, of invincible constancy, and unalienable kindness; and some examples have been seen of men who have continued faithful to their earliest choice, and whose affection has predominated over changes of fortune, and contrariety of opinion.

But these instances are memorable, because they are rare. The friendship which is to be practised or expected by common mortals, must take its rise from mutual pleasure, and must end when the power ceases of delighting each other.

Many accidents therefore may happen, by which the ardour of kindness will be abated, without criminal baseness or contemptible inconstancy on either part. To give pleasure is not always in our power; and little does he know himself, who believes that he can be always able to receive it.

Those who would gladly pass their days together may be separated by the different course of their affairs; and friendship, like love, is destroyed by long absence, though it may be encreased by short intermissions. What we have missed long enough to want it, we value more when it is regained; but that which has been lost till it is forgotten, will be found at last with little gladness, and with still less, if a substitute has supplied the place. A man deprived of the companion to whom he used to open his bosom, and with whom he shared the hours of leisure and merriment, feels the day at first hanging heavy on him; his difficulties oppress, and his doubts distract him; he sees time come and go without his wonted gratification, and all is sadness within and solitude about him. But this uneasiness never lasts long, necessity produces expedients, new amusements are discovered, and new conversation is admitted.

No expectation is more frequently disappointed, than that which naturally arises in the mind, from the prospect of meeting an old friend, after long separation. We expect the attraction to be revived, and the coalition to be renewed; no man considers how much alteration time has made in himself, and very few enquire what effect it has had upon others. The first hour convinces them, that the pleasure, which they have formerly enjoyed, is for ever at an end; different scenes have made different impressions, the opinions of both are changed, and that similitude of manners and sentiment is lost, which confirmed them both in the approbation of themselves.

Friendship is often destroyed by opposition of interest, not only by the ponderous and visible interest, which the desire of wealth and greatness forms and maintains, but by a thousand secret and slight competitions, scarcely known to the mind upon which they operate. There is scarcely any man without some favourite trifle which he values above greater attainments, some desire of petty praise which he cannot patiently suffer to be frustrated. This minute ambition is sometimes crossed before it is known, and sometimes defeated by wanton petulance; but such attacks are seldom made without the loss of friendship; for whoever has once found the vulnerable part will always be feared, and the resentment will burn on in secret of which shame hinders the discovery.

This, however, is a slow malignity, which a wise man will obviate as inconsistent with quiet, and a good man will repress as contrary to virtue; but human happiness is sometimes violated by some more sudden strokes.

A dispute begun in jest upon a subject which a moment before was on both parts regarded with careless indifference, is continued by the desire of conquest, till vanity kindles into rage, and opposition rankles into enmity. Against this hasty mischief I know not what security can be obtained; men will be sometimes surprised into quarrels, and though they might both hasten to reconciliation, as soon as their tumult had subsided, yet two minds will seldom be found together, which can at once subdue their discontent, or immediately enjoy the sweets of peace, without remembering the wounds of the conflict.

Friendship has other enemies. Suspicion is always hardening the cautious, and disgust repelling the delicate. Very slender differences will sometimes part those whom long reciprocation of civility or beneficence has united. Lonelove and Ranger retired into the country to enjoy the company of each other, and returned in six weeks cold and petulant; Ranger's pleasure was to walk in the fields, and Lonelove's to sit in a bower; each had complied with the other in his turn, and each was angry that compliance had been exacted.

The most fatal disease of friendship is gradual decay, or dislike hourly encreased by causes too slender for complaint, and too numerous for removal. Those who are angry may be reconciled; those who have been injured may receive a recompense; but when the desire of pleasing and willingness to be pleased is silently diminished, the renovation of friendship is hopeless; as, when the vital powers sink into languor, there is no longer any use of the physician.

— *reprinted from* The Works of Samuel Johnson, *Vol. II:* Idler and Adventurer, *ed. Bate, Bullitt, and Power (New Haven, Yale University Press, 1963); the title is not in the original*

James Boswell, who is considered to be the most outstanding biographer in English literature, attended Edinburgh High School and University and studied law at Edinburgh, Glasgow, and Utrecht. Following his graduation, he travelled extensively on the continent and became particularly interested in Corsica. He emerged on the literary scene with two publications about the Corsicans: An Account of Corsica (1768) and Essays in Favour of the Brave Corsicans (1769). In the years between 1772 and 1784 Boswell made frequent visits to London from Edinburgh to see Samuel Johnson, whom he had met in 1763. With Johnson he toured Scotland and the Hebrides; Boswell's account of this tour appeared in 1786 and was entitled Journal of a Tour to the Hebrides with Johnson, LL.D.

In 1788, Boswell moved to London, with his family, to practise law. He began to write his important biography of Johnson, for which he had kept a detailed diary. The book, entitled The Life of Samuel Johnson, appeared in 1791 and was acclaimed for its vivid and exact presentation of character. Boswell's personal journals were discovered in 1950.

(1740-1795)

JAMES BOSWELL

On Wealth, Poverty, and Merit

Rousseau's treatise on the inequality of mankind was at this time a fashionable topick. It gave rise to an observation by Mr. Dempster, that the advantages of fortune and rank were nothing to a wise man, who ought to value only merit. JOHNSON: "If man were a savage, living in the woods by himself, this might be true; but in civilized society we all depend upon each other, and our happiness is very much owing to the good opinion of mankind. Now, Sir, in civilized society, external advantages make us more respected. A man with a good coat upon his back meets with a better reception than he who has a bad one. Sir, you may analyse this, and say what is there in it? But that will avail you nothing, for it is a part of a general system. Pound St. Paul's Church into atoms, and consider any single atom; it, to be sure, is good for nothing: but, put all these atoms together, and you have St. Paul's Church. So it is with human felicity, which is made up of many ingredients, each of which may be shewn to be very significant. In civilized society, personal merit will not serve you so much as money will. Sir, you may make the experiment. Go into the street, and give one man a lecture on morality, and another a shilling, and see which will respect you most. If you wish only to support nature, Sir William Petty fixes your allowance at three pounds a year; but as times are much altered, let us call it six pounds. This sum will fill your belly, shelter you from the weather, and even get you a strong lasting coat, supposing it to be made of good bull's hide. Now, Sir, all beyond this is artificial, and is desired in order to obtain a greater degree of respect from our fellow-creatures. And, Sir, if six hundred pounds a year procure a man more consequence, and, of course, more happiness than six pounds a year, the same proportion will hold as to six thousand, and so on as far as opulence can be carried. Perhaps he who has a large fortune may not be so happy as he who has a small one; but that must proceed from other causes than from his having the large fortune: for, *caeteris paribus*, he who is rich in a civilized society, must be happier than he who is poor; as riches, if properly used, (and it is a man's own fault if they are not,) must be productive of the highest advantages. Money, to be sure, of itself is of no use; for its only use is to part with it. Rousseau, and all those who deal in paradoxes, are led away by a childish desire of novelty. When I was a boy, I used always to choose the wrong side of a debate, because most ingenious things, that is to say, most new things, could be said upon it. Sir, there is nothing for which you may not muster up more plausible arguments, than those which are urged against wealth and other external advantages. Why now, there is stealing; why should it be thought a crime? When we consider by what unjust methods property has been often acquired, and that what was unjustly got it must be unjust to keep, where is the harm in one man's taking the property of another from him? Besides, Sir, when we consider the bad use that many people make of their property, and how much better use the thief may make of it, it may be defended as a very allowable practice. Yet, Sir, the experience of mankind has discovered stealing to be so very bad a thing, that they make no scruple to hang a man for it. When I was running about this town a very poor fellow, I was a great arguer for the advantages of poverty; but I was, at the same time, very sorry to be poor. Sir, all the arguments which are brought to represent poverty as no evil, shew it to be evidently a great evil. You never find people labouring to convince you that you may live very happily upon a plentiful fortune.— So you hear people talking how miserable a King must be; and yet they all wish to be in his place.

— reprinted from Boswell's Life of Johnson, Vol. I: The Life, 1709-1765 (Oxford, Clarendon Press, 1934); our title is not in the original

William Hazlitt grew up in the village of Wem and received his early education exclusively from his father. A precocious child, Hazlitt published a newspaper article at the age of thirteen, and at the age of fifteen was enrolled in the Hackney Theological College to study for the Unitarian ministry. He left the College in 1797 and decided to pursue a career of art; to this end he spent some months in Paris where he studied painting. In 1805, he abandoned painting for a literary career and began to write articles for periodicals such as the Edinburgh Review, The Morning Chronicle, and The Examiner.

Hazlitt was well-known as a lecturer and published many of his lectures and essays: some deal with art and drama, including A Review of the English Stage and Conversations of James Northcote, Esq., R.A.; others deal with literary criticism, including Lectures on the English Poets, Lectures on the English Comic Writers, and Characters of Shakespeare's Plays. Hazlitt is important in the history of English literature as a critic. He is often grouped with writers of the Romantic movement because of his vivid imagination, his love of nature, and his high regard for the individual.

(1778-1830)

WILLIAM HAZLITT

On the Ignorance of the Learned

The description of persons who have the fewest ideas of all others are mere authors and readers. It is better to be able neither to read nor write than to be able to do nothing else. A lounger who is ordinarily seen with a book in his hand is (we may be almost sure) equally without the power or inclination to attend either to what passes around him or in his own mind. Such a one may be said to carry his understanding about with him in his pocket, or to leave it at home on his library shelves. He is afraid of venturing on any train of reasoning, or of striking out any observation that is not mechanically suggested to him by passing his eyes over certain legible characters; shrinks from the fatigue of thought, which, for want of practice, becomes insupportable to him; and sits down contented with an endless, wearisome succession of words and half-formed images, which fill the void of the mind, and continually efface one another. Learning is, in too many cases, but a foil to common sense; a substitute for true knowledge. Books are less often made use of as "spectacles" to look at nature with, than as blinds to keep out its strong light and shifting scenery from weak eyes and indolent dispositions. The book-worm wraps himself up in his web of verbal generalities, and sees only the glimmering shadows of things reflected from the minds of others. Nature *puts him out.* The impressions of real objects, stripped of the disguises of words and voluminous roundabout descriptions, are blows that stagger him; their variety distracts, their rapidity exhausts him; and he turns from the bustle, the noise, and glare, and whirling motion of the world about him (which he has not an eye to follow in its fantastic changes, nor an understanding to reduce to fixed principles), to the quiet monotony of the dead languages, and the less startling and more intelligible combinations of the letters of the alphabet. It is well, it is perfectly well. "Leave me to my repose," is the motto of the sleeping and the dead. You might as well ask the paralytic to leap from his chair and throw away his crutch, or, without a miracle, to "take up his bed and walk," as expect the learned reader to throw down his book and think for himself. He clings to it for his intellectual support; and his dread of being left to himself is like the horror of a vacuum. He can only breathe a learned atmosphere, as other men breathe common air. He is a borrower of sense. He has no ideas of his own, and must live on those of other people. The habit of supplying our ideas from foreign sources "enfeebles all internal strength of thought," as a course of dram-drinking destroys the tone of the stomach. The faculties of the mind, when not exerted, or when cramped by custom and authority, become listless, torpid, and unfit for the purposes of thought or action. Can we wonder at the languor and lassitude which is thus produced by a life of learned sloth and ignorance; by poring over lines and syllables that excite little more idea or interest than if they were the characters of an unknown tongue, till the eye closes on vacancy, and the book drops from the feeble hand! I would rather be a wood-cutter, or the meanest hind, that all day "sweats in the eye of Phoebus, and at night sleeps in Elysium," than wear out my life so, 'twixt dreaming and awake. The learned author differs from the learned student in this, that the one transcribes what the other reads. The learned are mere literary drudges. If you set them upon original composition, their heads turn, they don't know where they are. The indefatigable readers of books are like the everlasting copiers of pictures, who, when they attempt to do anything of their own, find they want an eye quick enough, a hand steady enough, and colours bright enough, to trade the living forms of nature.

Any one who has passed through the regular gradations of a classical education, and is not made a fool by it, may consider himself as having had a very narrow escape. It is an old remark, that boys who shine at school do not make the greatest figure when they grow up and come out into the world. The things, in fact, which a boy is set to learn at school, and on which his success depends, are things which do not require the exercise either of the highest or the most useful faculties of the mind. Memory (and that of the lowest kind) is the chief faculty called into play in conning over and repeating lessons by rote in grammar, in languages, in geography, arithmetic, &c., so that he who has the most of this technical memory, with the least turn for other things, which have a stronger and more natural claim upon his childish attention, will make the most forward school-boy. The jargon containing the definitions of the parts of speech, the rules for casing up an account, or the inflections of a Greek verb, can have no attraction to the tyro of ten years old, except as they are imposed as a task upon him by others, or from his feeling the want of sufficient relish or amusement in other things. A lad with a sickly constitution and no very active mind, who can just retain what is pointed out to him, and has neither sagacity to distinguish nor spirit to enjoy for himself, will generally be at the head of his form. An idler at school, on the other hand, is one who has high health and spirits, who has the free use of his limbs, with all his wits about him, who feels the circulation of his blood and the motion of his heart, who is ready to laugh and cry in a breath, and who had rather chase a ball or a butterfly, feel the open air in his face, look at the fields or the sky, follow a winding path, or enter with eagerness into all the little conflicts and interests of his acquaintances and friends, than doze over a musty spelling-book, repeat barbarous distichs after his master, sit so many hours pinioned to a writing-desk, and receive his reward for the loss of time and pleasure in paltry prize-medals at Christmas and Midsummer. There is indeed a degree of stupidity which prevents children from learning the usual lessons, or ever arriving at these puny academic honours. But what passes for stupidity is much oftener a want of interest, of a sufficient motive to fix the attention and force a reluctant application to the dry and unmeaning pursuits of school-learning. The best capacities are as much above this drudgery as the dullest are beneath it. Our men of the greatest genius have not been most distinguished for their acquirements at school or at the university.

"Th' enthusiast Fancy was a truant ever."

Gray and Collins were among the instances of this wayward disposition. Such persons do not think so highly of the advantages, nor can they submit their imaginations so servilely to the trammels of strict scholastic discipline. There is a certain kind and degree of intellect in which words take root, but into which things have not power to penetrate. A mediocrity of talent, with a certain slenderness of moral constitution, is the soil that produces the most brilliant specimens of successful prize-essayists and Greek epigrammatists. It should not be forgotten that the least respectable character among modern politicians was the cleverest boy at Eton.

Learning is the knowledge of that which is not generally known to others, and which we can only derive at second-hand from books or other artificial sources. The knowledge of that which is before us, or about us, which appeals to our experience, passions, and pursuits, to the bosoms and businesses of men, is not learning. Learning is the knowledge of that which none but the learned know. He is the most learned man who knows the most of what is farthest removed from common life and actual observation, that is of the least practical utility, and least liable to be brought to the test of experience, and that, having been handed down through the greatest number of intermediate stages, is the most full of uncertainty, difficulties, and contradictions. It is seeing with the eyes of others, hearing with their ears, and pinning our faith on their understandings. The learned man prides himself in the knowledge of names and dates, not of men or things. He thinks and cares nothing about his next-door neighbours, but he is deeply read in the tribes and castes of the Hindoos and Calmuc Tartars. He can hardly find his way into the next street, though he is acquainted with the exact dimensions of Constantinople and Pekin. He does not know whether his oldest acquaintance is a knave or a fool, but he can pronounce a pompous lecture on all the principal characters in history. He cannot tell whether an object is black or white, round or square, and yet he is a professed master of the laws of optics and the rules of perspective. He knows as much of what he talks about as a blind man does of colours. He cannot give a satisfactory answer to the plainest question, nor is he ever in the right in any one of his opinions upon any one matter of fact that really comes before him, and yet he gives himself out for an infallible judge on all those points, of which it is impossible that he or any other person living should know anything but by conjecture. He is expert in all the dead and in most of the living languages; but he can neither speak his own fluently, nor write it correctly. . . .

A mere scholar, who knows nothing but books, must be ignorant even of them. "Books do not teach the use of books." How should he know anything of a work who knows nothing of the subject of it? The learned pedant is conversant with books only as they are made of other books, and those again of others, without end. He parrots those who have parroted others. He can translate the same word into ten different languages, but he knows nothing of the *thing* which it means in any one of them. He stuffs his head with authorities built on authorities, with quotations quoted from quotations, while he locks up his senses, his understanding, and his heart. He is unacquainted with the maxims and manners of the world, he is to seek in the characters of individuals. He sees no beauty in the face of nature or of art. To him "the mighty world of eye and ear" is hid; and "knowledge," except at one entrance, "quite shut out." His pride takes part with his ignorance; and his self-importance rises with the number of things of which he does not know the value, and which he therefore despises as unworthy of his notice. . . . His ears are nailed to his books; and deadened with the sound of the Greek and Latin tongues, and the din and smithery of school-learning. Does he know anything more of poetry? He knows the number of feet in a verse, and of acts in a play; but of the soul or spirit he knows nothing. He can turn a Greek ode into English, or a Latin epigram into Greek verse, but whether either is worth the trouble he leaves to the critics. Does he

understand "the act and practique part of life" better than "the theorique"?
No. He knows no liberal or mechanic art, no trade or occupation, no game
of skill or chance. Learning "has no skill in surgery," in agriculture, in
building, in working in wood or in iron; it cannot make any instrument of
labour, or use it when made; it cannot handle the plough or the spade,
or the chisel or the hammer; it knows nothing of hunting or hawking, fishing
or shooting, of horses or dogs, of fencing or dancing, or cudgel-playing, or
bowls, or cards, or tennis, or anything else. The learned professor of all
arts and sciences cannot reduce any one of them to practice, though he may
contribute an account of them to an Encyclopaedia. He has not the use of
his hands or of his feet; he can neither run, nor walk, nor swim; and he considers all those who actually understand and can exercise any of these arts
of body or mind as vulgar and mechanical men,—though to know almost
any one of them in perfection requires long time and practice, with powers
originally fitted, and a turn of mind particularly devoted to them. It does
not require more than this to enable the learned candidate to arrive, by
painful study, at a doctor's degree and a fellowship, and to eat, drink, and
sleep the rest of his life!

The thing is plain. All that men really understand is confined to a very
small compass; to their daily affairs and experience; to what they have an
opportunity to know, and motives to study or practise. The rest is affectation
and imposture. The common people have the use of their limbs; for they
live by their labour or skill. They understand their own business and the
characters of those they have to deal with; for it is necessary that they
should. They have eloquence to express their passions, and wit at will to
express their contempt and provoke laughter. Their natural use of speech
is not hung up in monumental mockery, in an obsolete language; nor is
their sense of what is ludicrous, or readiness at finding out allusions to
express it, buried in collections of *Anas*. You will hear more good things
on the outside of a stagecoach from London to Oxford than if you were to
pass a twelvemonth with the undergraduates, or heads of colleges, of that
famous university; and more *home* truths are to be learnt from listening to
a noisy debate in an ale-house than from attending to a formal one in the
House of Commons. An elderly country gentlewoman will often know more
of character, and be able to illustrate it by more amusing anecdotes taken
from the history of what has been said, done, and gossiped in a country
town for the last fifty years, than the best blue-stocking of the age will be
able to glean from that sort of learning which consists in an acquaintance
with all the novels and satirical poems published in the same period. People
in towns, indeed, are woefully deficient in a knowledge of character, which
they see only *in the bust*, not as a whole-length. People in the country not
only know all that has happened to a man, but trace his virtues or vices,
as they do his features, in their descent through several generations, and solve

some contradiction in his behaviour by a cross in the breed half a century ago. The learned know nothing of the matter, either in town or country. Above all, the mass of society have common sense, which the learned in all ages want. The vulgar are in the right when they judge for themselves; they are wrong when they trust to their blind guides. The celebrated non-conformist divine, Baxter, was almost stoned to death by the good women of Kidderminster, for asserting from the pulpit that "hell was paved with infants' skulls"; but, by the force of argument, and of learned quotations from the Fathers, the reverend preacher at length prevailed over the scruples of his congregation, and over reason and humanity.

Such is the use which has been made of human learning. The labourers in this vineyard seem as if it was their object to confound all common sense, and the distinctions of good and evil, by means of traditional maxims and preconceived notions taken upon trust, and increasing in absurdity with increase of age. They pile hypothesis on hypothesis, mountain high, till it is impossible to come at the plain truth on any question. They see things, not as they are, but as they find them in books, and "wink and shut their apprehensions up," in order that they may discover nothing to interfere with their prejudices or convince them of their absurdity. It might be supposed that the height of human wisdom consisted in maintaining con-tradictions, and rendering nonsense sacred. There is no dogma, however fierce or foolish, to which these persons have not set their seals, and tried to impose it on the understandings of their followers, as the will of Heaven, clothed with all the terrors and sanctions of religion. How little has the human understanding been directed to find out the true and useful! How much ingenuity has been thrown away in the defence of creeds and systems! How much time and talents have been wasted in theological controversy, in law, in politics, in verbal criticism, in judicial astrology, and in finding out the art of making gold! What actual benefit do we reap from the writings of a Laud or a Whitgift, or of Bishop Bull or Bishop Waterland, or Prideaux' Connections, or Beausobre, or Calmet, or St. Augustine, or Puffendorf, or Vattel, or from the more literal but equally learned and unprofitable labours of Scaliger, Cardan, and Scioppius? How many grains of sense are there in their thousand folio or quarto volumes? What would the world lose if they were committed to the flames tomorrow? Or are they not already "gone to the vault of all the Capulets"? Yet all these were oracles in their time, and would have scoffed at you or me, at common sense and human nature, for differing with them. It is our turn to laugh now.

To conclude this subject. The most sensible people to be met with in society are men of business and of the world, who argue from what they see and know, instead of spinning cobweb distinctions of what things ought to be. Women have often more of what is called *good sense* than men. They have fewer pretensions; are less implicated in theories; and judge of objects more from their immediate and involuntary impression on the mind, and, therefore, more truly and naturally. They cannot reason wrong; for they do not reason at all. They do not think or speak by rule; and they have in general more eloquence and wit, as well as sense, on that account. By their wit, sense, and eloquence together, they generally contrive to govern their husbands. Their style, when they write to their friends (not for the book-sellers), is better than that of most authors. — Uneducated people have most exuberance of invention and the greatest freedom from prejudice. Shakespear's was evidently an uneducated mind, both in the freshness of his imagination and in the variety of his views; as Milton's was scholastic, in the texture both of his thoughts and feelings. Shakespear had not been accustomed to write themes at school in favour of virtue or against vice. To this we owe the unaffected but healthy tone of his dramatic morality. If we wish to know the force of human genius we should read Shakespear. If we wish to see the insignificance of human learning we may study his commentators.

— reprinted from Selected Essays of William Hazlitt, 1778-1830*, ed. Geoffrey Keynes (London: The Nonesuch Press, 1948)*

Charles Lamb grew up in the household of Samuel Salt, a lawyer to whom his father was a clerk. He was educated at Christ's Hospital, where he became a friend for life of Samuel Taylor Coleridge. From 1792 to 1825 Lamb was employed in the East India House, except for a brief period (1795-1796) when he was temporarily confined to a mental asylum. In 1796 he was forced to assume the lifelong responsibility of caring for his sister Mary after she stabbed their mother in a fit of madness.

Four of Lamb's sonnets appeared in a book of poetry published by Coleridge in 1796, and in 1798 more of his poetry appeared in a volume entitled Blank Verse, on which he collaborated with Charles Lloyd. After publishing The Tale of Rosamund Gray and Old Blind Margaret and two plays, he wrote, with his sister, Tales From Shakespeare and Mrs. Leicester's School, a collection of ten stories, supposedly autobiographical. With the publication in 1808 of Specimens of English Dramatic Poets Contemporary With Shakespeare, Lamb's reputation as a fine literary critic and essayist was established. Before moving from London to Edmonton, England, where he died, Lamb published other important works, including the famous Essays of Elia (1823) and, some years later, their sequel, Last Essays of Elia (1833).

(1775-1834)

CHARLES LAMB

Mrs. Battle's Opinions on Whist

"A clear fire, a clean hearth, and the rigour of the game." This was the celebrated *wish* of old Sarah Battle (now with God), who, next to her devotions, loved a good game of whist. She was none of your lukewarm gamesters, your half-and-half players, who have no objection to take a hand, if you want one to make up a rubber; who affirm that they have no pleasure in winning; that they like to win one game and lose another; that they can while away an hour very agreeably at a card-table, but are indifferent whether they play or no; and will desire an adversary, who has slipped a wrong card, to take it up and play another. These insufferable triflers are the curse of the table. One of these flies will spoil a whole pot. Of such it may be said that they do not play at cards, but only play at playing at them.

Sarah Battle was none of that breed. She detested them, as I do, from her heart and soul, and would not, save upon a striking emergency, willingly seat herself at the same table with them. She loved a thorough-paced partner, a determined enemy. She took, and gave, no concessions. She hated favours. She never made a revoke, nor ever passed it over in her adversary without exacting the utmost forfeiture. She fought a good fight: cut and thrust. She held not her good sword (her cards) "like a dancer." She sate bolt upright; and neither showed you her cards, nor desired to see yours. All people have their blind side—their superstitions; and I have heard her declare, under the rose, that hearts was her favourite suit.

I never in my life—and I knew Sarah Battle many of the best years of it— saw her take out her snuff-box when it was her turn to play; or snuff a candle in the middle of a game; or ring for a servant, till it was fairly over. She never introduced, or connived at, miscellaneous conversation during its process. As she emphatically observed, cards were cards; and if I ever saw unmingled distaste in her fine last-century countenance, it was at the airs of a young gentleman of a literary turn, who had been with difficulty persuaded to take a hand; and who, in his excess of candour, declared, that he thought there was no harm in unbending his mind now and then, after serious studies, in recreations of that kind! She could not bear to have her noble occupation, to which she wound up her faculties, considered in that light. It was her business, her duty, the thing she came into the world to do,—and she did it. She unbent her mind afterwards over a book. . . .

No inducement could ever prevail upon her to play at any game, where chance entered into the composition, *for nothing.* Chance, she would argue— and here again, admire the subtlety of her conclusion;—chance is nothing, but where something else depends upon it. It is obvious that cannot be *glory.* What rational cause of exultation could it give to a man to turn up size ace a hundred times together by himself? or before spectators, where no stake was depending?—Make a lottery of a hundred thousand tickets with but one fortunate number—and what possible principle of our nature, except stupid wonderment, could it gratify to gain that number as many times successively, without a prize? . . .

To those puny objectors against cards, as nurturing the bad passions, she would retort, that man is a gaming animal. He must be always trying to get the better in something or other:—that this passion can scarcely be more safely expended than upon a game at cards: that cards are a temporary illusion; in truth, a mere drama; for we do but *play* at being mightily con- cerned, where a few idle shillings are at stake, yet, during the illusion, we *are* as mightily concerned as those whose stake is crowns and kingdoms. They are a sort of dream-fighting; much ado; great battling, and little blood- shed; mighty means for disproportioned ends; quite as diverting, and a great deal more innoxious, than many of those more serious *games* of life, which men play, without esteeming them to be such. . . .

—*this and the following selection reprinted from* <u>The Complete Works and Letters of Charles Lamb</u> *(New York, Random House, Inc., 1935)*

Letter to William Wordsworth

Jan. 30, 1801

I ought before this to have replied to your very kind invitation into Cumberland. With you and your sister I could gang anywhere; but I am afraid whether I shall ever be able to afford so desperate a journey. Separate from the pleasure of your company, I don't much care if I never see a mountain in my life. I have passed all my days in London, until I have formed as many and intense local attachments as any of you mountaineers can have done with dead nature. The lighted shops of the Strand and Fleet Street; the innumerable trades, tradesmen, and customers, coaches, waggons, playhouses; all the bustle and wickedness round about Covent Garden; the very women of the Town; the watchmen, drunken scenes, rattles; life awake, if you awake, at all hours of the night; the impossibility of being dull in Fleet Street; the crowds, the very dirt and mud, the sun shining upon houses and pavements, the print shops, the old bookstalls, parsons cheapening books, coffee-houses, steams of soups from kitchens, the pantomimes—London itself a pantomime and a masquerade—all these things work themselves into my mind, and feed me, without a power of satiating me. The wonder of these sights impels me into night-walks about her crowded streets, and I often shed tears in the motley Strand from fulness of joy at so much life. All these emotions must be strange to you; so are your rural emotions to me. But consider, what must I have been doing all my life, not to have lent great portions of my heart with usury to such scenes?

My attachments are all local, purely local. I have no passion (or have had none since I was in love, and then it was the spurious engendering of poetry and books) for groves and valleys. The rooms where I was born, the furniture which has been before my eyes all my life, a book-case which has followed me about like a faithful dog (only exceeding him in knowledge), wherever I have moved, old chairs, old tables, streets, squares, where I have sunned myself, my old school—these are my mistresses. Have I not enough, without your mountains? I do not envy you. I should pity you, did I not know that the mind will make friends of anything. Your sun, and moon, and skies, and hills, and lakes, affect me no more, or scarcely come to me in more venerable characters, than as a gilded room with tapestry and tapers, where I might live with handsome visible objects. I consider the clouds above me but as a roof beautifully painted, but unable to satisfy the mind: and at last, like the pictures of the apartment of a connoisseur, unable to afford him any longer a pleasure. So fading upon me, from disuse, have been the beauties of Nature, as they have been confinedly called; so ever fresh, and green, and warm are all the inventions of men, and assemblies of men in this great city. I should certainly have laughed with dear Joanna.

Give my kindest love, and my sister's, to D. and yourself; and a kiss from me to little Barbara Lewthwaite. Thank you for liking my play.

C. L.

John Ruskin, who was the son of a wealthy wine merchant, travelled extensively before entering Christ Church College, Oxford, in 1836. He graduated in 1842 and in 1843 made his debut as an art critic with the publication of the first volume of Modern Painters. Four additional volumes were subsequently published in 1846, 1856, and 1860. His literary reputation was established by these books and others, including The Seven Lamps of Architecture (1849) and The Stones of Venice (1851-1853).

After 1860, Ruskin became interested in the social problems of his age and was an ardent advocate of reform. He wrote many treatises and pamphlets which expounded his philosophies; noteworthy among them were Sesame and Lilies (1865) and The Crown of Wild Olive (1866). From 1870 to 1879 and from 1883 to 1884 he lectured at Oxford, and in 1885 began his last book, *Praeterita. An autobiography, it was published at intervals from 1885 to 1889, but was unfinished at the time of his death.*

(1819-1900)

JOHN RUSKIN

Turner's "Slave Ship"

But, I think, the noblest sea that Turner has ever painted, and, if so, the noblest certainly ever painted by man, is that of the Slave Ship, the chief Academy picture of the Exhibition of 1840. It is a sunset on the Atlantic, after prolonged storm; but the storm is partially lulled, and the torn and streaming rain-clouds are moving in scarlet lines to lose themselves in the hollow of the night. The whole surface of sea included in the picture is divided into two ridges of enormous swell, not high, nor local, but a low broad heaving of the whole ocean, like the lifting of its bosom by deep-drawn breath after the torture of the storm. Between these two ridges the fire of the sunset falls along the trough of the sea, dyeing it with an awful but glorious light, the intense and lurid splendour which burns like gold and bathes like blood. Along this fiery path and valley, the tossing waves by which the swell of the sea is restlessly divided, lift themselves in dark, indefinite, fantastic forms, each casting a faint and ghastly shadow behind it along the illumined foam. They do not rise everywhere, but three or four together in wild groups, fitfully and furiously, as the under strength of the swell compels or permits them; leaving between them treacherous spaces of level and whirling water, now lighted with green and lamp-like fire, now flashing back the gold of the declining sun, now fearfully dyed from above with the undistinguishable images of the burning clouds, which fall upon them in flakes of crimson and scarlet, and give to the reckless waves the added motion of their own fiery flying. Purple and blue, the lurid shadows of the hollow breakers are cast upon the mist of the night, which gathers cold and low, advancing like the shadow of death upon the guilty ship as it labours amidst the lightning of the sea, its thin masts written upon the sky in lines of blood, girded with condemnation in that fearful hue which signs the sky with horror, and mixes its flaming flood with the sunlight, and, cast far along the desolate heave of the sepulchral waves, incarnadines the multitudinous sea.

I believe, if I were reduced to rest Turner's immortality upon any single work, I should choose this. Its daring conception, ideal in the highest sense of the word, is based on the purest truth, and wrought out with the concentrated knowledge of a life; its colours absolutely perfect, not one false or morbid hue in any part or line, and so modulated that every square inch of canvas is a perfect composition; its drawing as accurate as fearless; the ship buoyant, behind, and full of motion; its tones as true as they are wonderful; and the whole picture dedicated to the most sublime of subjects and impressions (completing thus the perfect system of all truth, which we have shown to be formed by Turner's works)—the power, majesty, and deathfulness of the open, deep, illimitable sea.

— reprinted from The Works of John Ruskin, *ed. E. T. Cook and Alexander Wedderburn, Vol. II:* Modern Painters, *Part II, Sec. V, Ch. 3 (London, George Allen, 1903)*

In 1861, Abraham Lincoln became the sixteenth President of the United States and retained that office until his assassination by John Wilkes Booth in 1865. As a political figure, Lincoln is well remembered for the Emancipation Proclamation of 1862 which liberated the slaves; as a literary figure, he is best remembered for his letters and speeches which reflect a richness in thought and a perceptive awareness of the contemporary scene during his presidency. His most famous speech is The Gettysburg Address, presented in November, 1863, after the Battle of Gettysburg. Lincoln has been immortalized in poetry by Walt Whitman, in plays by John Drinkwater and Robert Sherwood, and in novels by Honore Morrow, Upton Sinclair, and Edward Eggleston.

Lincoln's early life and political activities are described in the autobiographical essay that follows. He sent this short sketch of his life to J. W. Fell on December 20, 1859, in order that it might be used for campaign purposes. Lincoln was campaigning for the presidency at the time.

(*1809-1865*)

ABRAHAM LINCOLN

Autobiographical Sketch

I was born February 12, 1809, in Hardin County, Kentucky. My parents were both born in Virginia, of undistinguished families—second families, perhaps I should say. My mother, who died in my tenth year, was of a family of the name of Hanks, some of whom now reside in Adams, and others in Macon County, Illinois. My paternal grandfather, Abraham Lincoln, emigrated from Rockingham County, Virginia, to Kentucky about 1781 or 1782, where a year or two later he was killed by the Indians, not in battle, but by stealth, when he was laboring to open a farm in the forest. His ancestors, who were Quakers, went to Virginia from Berks County, Pennsylvania. An effort to identify them with the New England family of the same name ended in nothing more definite than a similarity of Christian names in both families, such as Enoch, Levi, Mordecai, Solomon, Abraham, and the like.

My father, at the death of his father, was but six years of age, and he grew up literally without education. He removed from Kentucky to what is now Spencer County, Indiana, in my eighth year. We reached our new home about the time the state came into the Union. It was a wild region, with many bears and other wild animals still in the woods. There I grew up. There were some schools, so called, but no qualification was ever required of a teacher beyond "readin', writin', and cipherin'," to the rule of three. If a straggler supposed to understand Latin happened to sojourn in the neighborhood, he was looked upon as a wizard. There was absolutely nothing to excite ambition for education. Of course, when I came of age I did not know much. Still, somehow, I could read, write, and cipher to the rule of three, but that was all. I have not been to school since. The little advance I now have upon this store of education, I have picked up from time to time under the pressure of necessity.

I was raised to farm work, which I continued till I was twenty-two. At twenty-one I came to Illinois, Macon County. Then I got to New Salem, at that time in Sangamon, now in Menard County, where I remained a year as a sort of clerk in a store. Then came the Black Hawk War; and I was elected a captain of volunteers, a success which gave me more pleasure than any I have had since. I went the campaign, was elated, ran for the legislature the same year (1832), and was beaten—the only time I ever have been beaten by the people. The next and three succeeding biennial elections I was elected to the legislature. I was not a candidate afterward. During this legislative period I had studied law, and removed to Springfield to practise it. In 1846 I was once elected to the lower House of Congress. Was not a candidate for re-election. From 1849 to 1854, both inclusive, practised law more assiduously than ever before. Always a Whig in politics; and generally on the Whig electoral tickets, making active canvasses. I was losing interest in politics when the repeal of the Missouri compromise aroused me again. What I have done since then is pretty well known.

If any personal description of me is thought desirable, it may be said I am, in height, six feet four inches, nearly; lean in flesh, weighing on an average one hundred and eighty pounds; dark complexion, with coarse black hair and gray eyes. No other marks or brands recollected.

— *reprinted from <u>Complete Works of Abraham Lincoln</u>, ed. J. Nicolay and J. Hay, Vol. V (New York, The Tandy-Thomas Co., 1905)*

Henry David Thoreau received his university education at Harvard and, after graduating in 1837, taught school with his brother in Concord, Massachusetts. He soon decided upon a literary career, however, and gave up teaching. From 1841 to 1843 he lived with Ralph Waldo Emerson and under his influence became a member of the Transcendental Club; during this time he also contributed articles to several magazines.

Because of his revolutionary spirit and his belief in the importance of the individual, Thoreau became a recluse and lived alone in a hut at the edge of Walden Pond from July 4, 1845, to September 6, 1847. (His solitary sojourn was interrupted only when he was imprisoned for one day for refusing to pay a poll tax.) He wrote his best-known work, <u>Walden, or Life in the Woods</u>, during this time. Like his other well-known works, (<u>A Week on the Concord and Merrimac Rivers</u>, <u>Excursions in Field and Forest</u>, <u>The Maine Woods</u>, and <u>Cape Cod</u>), <u>Walden</u> reflects Thoreau's deep love of nature and illustrates his acute sense of observation.

(1817-1862)

HENRY DAVID THOREAU

He returned from Walden to Concord and wrote his lengthy journals and an unpublished study of the North American Indian before succumbing to tuberculosis in 1862.

An excerpt from "Walden"

When first I took up my abode in the woods, that is, began to spend my nights as well as days there, which, by accident, was on Independence Day, or the Fourth of July, 1845, my house was not finished for winter, but was merely a defence against the rain, without plastering or chimney, the walls being of rough, weather-stained boards, with wide chinks, which made it cool at night. The upright white hewn studs and freshly planed door and window casings gave it a clean and airy look, especially in the morning, when its timbers were saturated with dew, so that I fancied that by noon some sweet gum would exude from them. To my imagination it retained throughout the day more or less of this auroral character, reminding me of a certain house on a mountain which I had visited a year before. This was an airy and unplastered cabin, fit to entertain a travelling god, and where a goddess might trail her garments. The winds which passed over my dwelling were such as sweep over the ridges of mountains, bearing the broken strains, or celestial parts only, of terrestrial music. The morning wind forever blows, the poem of creation is uninterrupted; but few are the ears that hear it. Olympus is but the outside of the earth everywhere. . . .

I was seated by the shore of a small pond, about a mile and a half south of the village of Concord and somewhat higher than it, in the midst of an extensive wood between that town and Lincoln, and about two miles south of that our only field known to fame, Concord Battle Ground; but I was so low in the woods that the opposite shore, half a mile off, like the rest, covered with wood, was my most distant horizon. For the first week, whenever I looked out on the pond it impressed me like a tarn high up on the side of a mountain, its bottom far above the surface of other lakes, and, as the sun arose, I saw it throwing off its nightly clothing of mist, and here and there, by degrees, its soft ripples or its smooth reflecting surface was revealed, while the mists, like ghosts, were stealthily withdrawing in every direction into the woods, as at the breaking up of some nocturnal conventicle. The very dew seemed to hang upon the trees later into the day than usual, as on the sides of mountains. . . .

Though the view from my door was still more contracted, I did not feel crowded or confined in the least. There was pasture enough for my imagination. The low shrub oak plateau, to which the opposite shore arose, stretched away toward the prairies of the West and the steppes of Tartary, affording ample room for all the roving families of men. "There are none happy in the world but beings who enjoy freely a vast horizon,"—said Damodara, when his herds required new and larger pastures. . . .

Every morning was a cheerful invitation to make my life of equal simplicity, and I may say innocence, with Nature herself. I have been as sincere a worshipper of Aurora as the Greeks. I got up early and bathed in the pond; that was a religious exercise, and one of the best things which I did. They say that characters were engraven on the bathing tub of King Tching-thang to this effect: "Renew thyself completely each day; do it again, and again, and forever again." I can understand that. Morning brings back the heroic ages. I was as much affected by the faint hum of a mosquito making its invisible and unimaginable tour through my apartment at earliest dawn, when I was sitting with door and windows open, as I could be by any trumpet that ever sang of fame. It was Homer's requiem; itself an Iliad and Odyssey in the air, singing its own wrath and wanderings. There was something cosmical about it; a standing advertisement, till forbidden, of the everlasting vigor and fertility of the world. The morning, which is the most memorable season of the day, is the awakening hour. Then there is least somnolence in us; and for an hour, at least, some part of us awakes which slumbers all the rest of the day and night. Little is to be expected of that day, if it can be called a day, to which we are not awakened by our Genius, but by the mechanical nudgings of some servitor, are not awakened by our newly acquired force and aspirations from within, accompanied by the undulations of celestial music, instead of factory bells, and a fragrance filling the air—to a higher life than we fell asleep from; and thus the darkness bear its fruit, and prove itself to be good, no less than the light. That man who does not believe that each day contains an earlier, more sacred, and auroral hour than he has yet profaned, has despaired of life, and is pursuing a descending and darkening way. After a partial cessation of his sensuous life, the soul of man, or its organs rather, are reinvigorated each day, and his Genius tries again what noble life it can make. All memorable events, I should say, transpire in morning time and in a morning atmosphere. The Vedas say, "All intelligences awake with the morning." Poetry and art, and the fairest and most memorable of the actions of men, date from such an hour. All poets and heroes, like Memnon, are the children of Aurora, and emit their music at sunrise. To him whose elastic and vigorous thought keeps pace with the sun, the day is a perpetual morning. It matters not what the clocks say or the attitudes and labors of men. Morning is when I am awake and there is a dawn in me. Moral reform is the effort to throw off sleep. Why is it that men give so poor an account of their day if they have not been slumbering? They are not such poor calculators. If they had not been overcome with drowsiness, they would have performed something. The millions are awake enough for physical labor; but only one in a million is awake enough for effective intellectual exertion, only one in a hundred millions to a poetic or divine life. To be awake is to be alive. I have never yet met a man who was quite awake. How could I have looked him in the face? . . .

I went to the woods because I wished to live deliberately, to front only the essential facts of life, and see if I could not learn what it had to teach, and not, when I came to die, discover that I had not lived. I did not wish to live what was not life, living is so dear; nor did I wish to practise resignation, unless it was quite necessary. I wanted to live deep and suck out all the marrow of life, to live so sturdily and Spartan-like as to put to rout all that was not life, to cut a broad swath and shave close, to drive life into a corner, and reduce it to its lowest terms, and, if it proved to be mean, why then to get the whole and genuine meanness of it, and publish its meanness to the world; or if it were sublime, to know it by experience, and be able to give a true account of it in my next excursion. For most men, it appears to me, are in a strange uncertainty about it, whether it is of the devil or of God, and have *somewhat hastily* concluded that it is the chief end of man here to "glorify God and enjoy Him forever."

Still we live meanly, like ants; though the fable tells us that we were long ago changed into men; like pygmies we fight with cranes; it is error upon error, and clout upon clout, and our best virtue has for its occasion a superfluous and evitable wretchedness. Our life is frittered away by detail. An honest man has hardly need to count more than his ten fingers, or in extreme cases he may add his ten toes, and lump the rest. Simplicity, simplicity, simplicity! I say, let your affairs be as two or three, and not a hundred or a thousand; instead of a million count half a dozen, and keep your accounts on your thumb-nail. In the midst of this chopping sea of civilized life, such are the clouds and storms and quicksands and thousand-and-one items to be allowed for, that a man has to live, if he would not founder and go to the bottom and not make his port at all, by dead reckoning, and he must be a great calculator indeed who succeeds. Simplify, simplify. Instead of three meals a day, if it be necessary eat but one; instead of a hundred dishes, five; and reduce other things in proportion. Our life is like a German Confederacy, made up of petty states, with its boundary forever fluctuating, so that even a German cannot tell you how it is bounded at any moment. The nation itself, with all its so-called internal improvements, which, by the way, are all external and superficial, is just such an unwieldy and overgrown establishment, cluttered with furniture and tripped up by its own traps, ruined by luxury and heedless expense, by want of calculation and a worthy aim, as the million households in the land; and the only cure for it, as for them, is in a rigid economy, a stern and more than Spartan simplicity of life and elevation of purpose. It lives too fast. Men think that it is essential that the *Nation* have commerce, and export ice, and talk through a telegraph, and ride thirty miles an hour, without a doubt, whether *they* do or not; but whether we should live like baboons or like men, is a little uncertain. If we do not get out sleepers, and forge rails, and devote days and nights to the work, but go to tinkering upon our *lives* to improve *them*, who will build railroads? And if railroads are not built, how shall we get to Heaven in season? But if we stay at home and mind our business, who will want railroads? We do not ride on the railroad; it rides upon us. Did you ever think what those sleepers are that underlie the railroad? Each one is a man, an Irishman, or a Yankee man. The rails are laid on them, and they are covered with sand, and the cars run smoothly over them. They are sound sleepers, I assure you. And every few years a new lot is laid down and run over; so that, if some have the pleasure of riding on a rail, others have the misfortune to be ridden upon. And when they run over a man that is walking in his sleep, a supernumerary sleeper in the wrong position, and wake him up, they suddenly stop the cars, and make a hue and cry about it, as if this were an exception. I am glad to know that it takes a gang of men for every five miles to keep the sleepers down and level in their beds as it is, for this is a sign that they may sometime get up again.

Why should we live with such hurry and waste of life? We are determined to be starved before we are hungry. Men say that a stitch in time saves nine, and so they take a thousand stitches today to save nine tomorrow. As for *work*, we haven't any of any consequence. We have the Saint Vitus' dance, and cannot possibly keep our heads still. If I should only give a few pulls at the parish bell-rope, as for a fire, that is, without setting the bell, there is hardly a man on his farm in the outskirts of Concord, notwithstanding that press of engagements which was his excuse so many times this morning, nor a boy nor a woman, I might almost say, but would forsake all and follow that sound, not mainly to save property from the flames, but, if we will confess the truth, much more to see it burn, since burn it must, and we, be it known, did not set it on fire, — or to see it put out, and have a hand in it, if that is done as handsomely; yes, even if it were the parish church itself. Hardly a man takes a half-hour's nap after dinner, but when he wakes he holds up his head and asks, "What's the news?" as if the rest of mankind had stood his sentinels. Some give directions to be waked every half-hour, doubtless for no other purpose; and then, to pay for it, they tell what they have dreamed. After a night's sleep the news is as indispensable as the breakfast. "Pray, tell me anything new that has happened to a man anywhere on this globe," — and he reads it over his coffee and rolls, that a man has had his eyes gouged out this morning on the Wachito River; never dreaming the while that he lives in the dark unfathomed mammoth cave of this world, and has but the rudiment of an eye himself.

For my part, I could easily do without the post-office. I think that there are very few important communications made through it. To speak critically, I never received more than one or two letters in my life—I wrote this some years ago — that were worth the postage. The penny-post is, commonly, an institution through which you seriously offer a man that penny for his thoughts which is so often safely offered in jest. And I am sure that I never read any memorable news in a newspaper. If we read of one man robbed, or murdered, or killed by accident, or one house burned, or one vessel wrecked, or one steamboat blown up, or one cow run over on the Western Railroad, or one mad dog killed, or one lot of grasshoppers in the winter,—we never need read of another. One is enough. If you are acquainted with the principle, what do you care for a myriad instances and applications? To a philosopher all *news*, as it is called, is gossip, and they who edit and read it are old women over their tea. Yet not a few are greedy after this gossip. There was such a rush, as I hear, the other day at one of the offices to learn the foreign news by the last arrival, that several large squares of plate glass belonging to the establishment were broken by the pressure,—news which I seriously think a ready wit might write a twelve-month, or twelve years, beforehand with sufficient accuracy. As for Spain, for instance, if you know how to throw in Don Carlos and the Infanta, and Don Pedro and Seville and Granada, from time to time in the right proportions,— they may have changed the names a little since I saw the papers, — and serve up a bull-fight when other entertainments fail, it will be true to the letter, and give us as good an idea of the exact state or ruin of things in Spain as the most succinct and lucid reports under this head in the newspapers: and as for England, almost the last significant scrap of news from that quarter was the revolution of 1649; and if you have learned the history of her crops for an average year, you never need attend to that thing again, unless your speculations are of a merely pecuniary character.

If one may judge who rarely looks into the newspapers, nothing new does ever happen in foreign parts, a French revolution not excepted.

What news! how much more important to know what that is which was never old! "Kieou-he-yu (great dignitary of the state of Wei) sent a man to Khoung-tseu to know his news. Khoung-tseu caused the messenger to be seated near him, and questioned him in these terms: What is your master doing? The messenger answered with respect: My master desires to diminish the number of his faults, but he cannot come to the end of them. The messenger being gone, the philosopher remarked: What a worthy messenger! What a worthy messenger!" The preacher, instead of vexing the ears of drowsy farmers on their day of rest at the end of the week,—for Sunday is the fit conclusion of an ill-spent week, and not the fresh and brave beginning of a new one,—with this one other draggle-tail of a sermon, should shout with thundering voice, "Pause! Avast! Why so seeming fast, but deadly slow?" . . .

Time is but the stream I go a-fishing in. I drink at it; but while I drink I see the sandy bottom and detect how shallow it is. Its thin current slides away, but eternity remains. I would drink deeper; fish in the sky, whose bottom is pebbly with stars. I cannot count one. I know not the first letter of the alphabet. I have always been regretting that I was not as wise as the day I was born. The intellect is a cleaver; it discerns and rifts its way into the secret of things. I do not wish to be any more busy with my hands than is necessary. My head is hands and feet. I feel all my best faculties concentrated in it. My instinct tells me that my head is an organ for burrowing, as some creatures use their snout and fore paws, and with it I would mine and burrow my way through these hills. I think that the richest vein is somewhere hereabouts; so by the divining-rod and thin rising vapors I judge; and here I will begin to mine.

— *reprinted from* <u>Walden</u>, *Rinehart edition, ed. Norman H. Pearson (New York, Holt, Rinehart and Winston, Inc., Publishers, 1948); with permission*

Samuel Langhorne Clemens was born in Florida, Missouri, and spent his boyhood in the small town of Hannibal on the shore of the Mississippi River. Some of his experiences on his uncle's farm during these early years are described in the autobiographical essay that follows.

His boyhood freedom ended when he was twelve years old. The death of his father and the resulting poverty of the family forced him to leave school and begin to learn a trade. After a brief apprenticeship as a printer's assistant, he worked as a typesetter on his brother's newspaper, the _Hannibal Journal_, to which he occasionally contributed his own poems and anecdotes.

When he was seventeen, he left Hannibal and for the next twenty years rambled about the United States, spent some time in Europe, and engaged in a variety of occupations. He was successively a printer on several newspapers in New York State, an apprentice steamboat pilot on the Mississippi, a volunteer soldier in the Civil War, a journalist in Nevada and San Francisco, and a publisher of the _Buffalo Express_.

While reporting for the _Territorial Enterprise_ in Virginia City, Nevada, he adopted the pen name, "Mark Twain," a term he had heard frequently when he was a cub-pilot on the Mississippi. It was the call of the man measuring the depth of that part of the river through which the river steamer was passing.

His varied experiences, the stories he heard during his travels, and the articles he wrote for newspapers and magazines, provided the material for several of his books. _Life on the Mississippi_ describes Clemens' efforts to become a famous river pilot so that he "could come home in glory" to his native town. _Roughing It_ pictures the vitality of the West, and recaptures the activity and excitement in Carson City when it was a great gold-mining centre, where fortunes were made and lost overnight. _The Innocents Abroad_ and _A Tramp Abroad_ tell of his travels through Europe, picture some of the famous buildings in France and Italy, and digress occasionally to describe the strange European customs and the weird behavior of American tourists.

Though these books and his story of "the celebrated jumping frog" brought Clemens wide recognition during his lifetime, his best-known works are two novels. The first is _Tom Sawyer_, which tells of boyhood adventures in a town very much like Hannibal. The second, considered one of the great novels of all time, is _Huckleberry Finn_. In this story of Huck's journey down the Mississippi on a raft, Mark Twain lets us see the good and evil in human beings as their behavior is observed through the eyes of a boy and described in the language that a boy might use.

It is interesting that Mark Twain, who had had only six years' formal education, became America's best-known writer. Many of the qualities that contributed to his success are revealed in the selection that follows. The student may note his perceptive *observation of human behavior, his sensitivity to his surroundings, his lucid prose, his ability to range in tone from serious to light and whimsical, and an imagination that would permit him to "move a state if the exigencies of literature required it."*

(*1835-1910*)

MARK TWAIN

An excerpt from "Autobiography"

My uncle, John A. Quarles, was a farmer and his place was in the country four miles from Florida. He had eight children and fifteen or twenty Negroes and was also fortunate in other ways, particularly in his character. I have not come across a better man than he was. I was his guest for two or three months every year, from the fourth year after we removed to Hannibal till I was eleven or twelve years old. I have never consciously used him or his wife in a book, but his farm has come very handy to me in literature once or twice. In *Huck Finn* and in *Tom Sawyer, Detective* I moved it down to Arkansas. It was all of six hundred miles but it was no trouble; it was not a very large farm, five hundred acres perhaps, but I could have done it if it had been twice as large. And as for the morality of it, I cared nothing for that; I would move a state if the exigencies of literature required it.

It was a heavenly place for a boy, that farm of my uncle John's. The house was a double log one with a spacious floor (roofed in) connecting it with the kitchen. In the summer the table was set in the middle of that shady and breezy floor, and the sumptuous meals—well, it makes me cry to think of them. Fried chicken, roast pig, wild and tame turkeys, ducks and geese, venison just killed, squirrels, rabbits, pheasants, partridges, prairie-chickens, biscuits, hot batter-cakes, hot buckwheat cakes, hot "wheat bread," hot rolls, hot corn pone; fresh corn boiled on the ear, succotash, butter beans, string beans, tomatoes, peas, Irish potatoes, sweet potatoes; buttermilk, sweet milk; "clabber"; watermelons, muskmelons, cantaloupes —all fresh from the garden—apple pie, peach pie, pumpkin pie, apple dumplings, peach cobbler—I can't remember the rest. The way that the things were cooked was perhaps the main splendor, particularly a certain few of the dishes. For instance the corn bread, the hot biscuits and wheat bread, and the fried chicken. These things have never been properly cooked in the North—in fact no one there is able to learn the art, so far as

— pp. 96-113 from Mark Twain's Autobiography, 2 vols.; copyright 1924, by Clara Gabrilowitsch, renewed 1952 by Clara Clemens Samossoud; reprinted by permission of Harper & Row, Publishers

my experience goes. The North thinks it knows how to make corn bread but this is mere superstition. Perhaps no bread in the world is quite so good as Southern corn bread, and perhaps no bread in the world is quite so bad as the Northern imitation of it. The North seldom tries to fry chicken and this is well; the art cannot be learned north of the line of Mason and Dixon, nor anywhere in Europe. This is not hearsay; it is experience that is speaking. In Europe it is imagined that the custom of serving various kinds of bread blazing hot is "American" but that is too broad a spread; it is custom in the South but is much less than that in the North. In the North and in Europe hot bread is considered unhealthy. This is probably another fussy superstition, like the European superstition that ice-water is unhealthy. Europe does not need ice-water and does not drink it; and yet notwithstanding this its word for it is better than ours, because it describes it, whereas ours doesn't. Europe calls it "iced" water. Our word describes water made from melted ice—a drink which has a characterless taste and which we have but little acquaintance with.

It seems a pity that the world should throw away so many good things merely because they are unwholesome. I doubt if God has given us any refreshment which, taken in moderation, is unwholesome, except microbes. Yet there are people who strictly deprive themselves of each and every eatable, drinkable, and smokable which has in any way acquired a shady reputation. They pay this price for health. And health is all they get for it. How strange it is. It is like paying out your whole fortune for a cow that has gone dry.

The farm-house stood in the middle of a very large yard and the yard was fenced on three sides with rails and on the rear side with high palings; against these stood the smoke-house; beyond the palings was the orchard; beyond the orchard were the Negro quarter and the tobacco fields. The front yard was entered over a stile made of sawed-off logs of graduated heights; I do not remember any gate. In a corner of the front yard were a dozen lofty hickory trees and a dozen black walnuts, and in the nutting season riches were to be gathered there.

Down a piece, abreast the house, stood a little log cabin against the rail fence; and there the woody hill fell sharply away, past the barns, the corn-crib, the stables, and the tobacco-curing house, to a limpid brook which sang along over its gravelly bed and curved and frisked in and out and here and there and yonder in the deep shade of overhanging foliage and vines—a divine place for wading, and it had swimming pools, too, which were forbidden to us and therefore much frequented by us. For we were little Christian children and had early been taught the value of forbidden fruit.

In the little log cabin lived a bedridden white-headed slave woman whom we visited daily and looked upon with awe, for we believed she was upward of a thousand years old and had talked with Moses. The younger Negroes credited these statistics and had furnished them to us in good faith. We accommodated all the details which came to us about her, and so we believed that she had lost her health in the long desert trip coming out of Egypt and had never been able to get it back again. She had a round bald place on the crown of her head, and we used to creep around and gaze at it in reverent silence and reflect that it was caused by fright through seeing Pharaoh drowned. We called her "Aunt" Hannah, Southern fashion. She was superstitious, like the other Negroes; also, like them, she was deeply religious. Like them, she had great faith in prayer and employed it in all ordinary exigencies, but not in cases where a dead certainty of result was urgent. Whenever witches were around she tied up the remnant of her wool in little tufts with white thread, and this promptly made the witches impotent.

All the Negroes were friends of ours and with those of our own age we were in effect comrades. I say in effect, using the phrase as a modification. We were comrades and yet not comrades; color and condition interposed a subtle line which both parties were conscious of and which rendered complete fusion impossible. We had a faithful and affectionate good friend, ally, and adviser in "Uncle Dan'l," a middle-aged slave whose head was the best one in the Negro quarter, whose sympathies were wide and warm, and whose heart was honest and simple and knew no guile. He has served me well these many, many years. I have not seen him for more than half a century, and yet spiritually I have had his welcome company a good part of that time and have staged him in books under his own name and as Jim and carted him all around, to Hannibal, down the Mississippi on a raft, and even across the Desert of Sahara in a balloon—and he has endured it all with the patience and friendliness and loyalty which were his birthright. It was on the farm that I got my strong liking for his race and my appreciation of certain of its fine qualities. This feeling and this estimate have stood the test of sixty years and more, and have suffered no impairment. The black face is as welcome to me now as it was then.

In my school-boy days I had no aversion to slavery. I was not aware that there was anything wrong about it. No one arraigned it in my hearing; the local papers said nothing against it; the local pulpit taught us that God approved it, that it was a holy thing, and that the doubter need only look in the Bible if he wished to settle his mind—and then the texts were read aloud to us to make the matter sure; if the slaves themselves had an aversion to slavery, they were wise and said nothing. In Hannibal we seldom saw a slave misused; on the farm, never.

There was, however, one small incident of my boyhood days which touched this matter and it must have meant a good deal to me or it would not have stayed in my memory, clear and sharp, vivid and shadowless, all these slow-drifting years. We had a little slave boy whom we had hired from some one, there in Hannibal. He was from the Eastern Shore of Maryland and had been brought away from his family and his friends, halfway across the American continent, and sold. He was a cheery spirit, innocent and gentle, and the noisiest creature that ever was perhaps. All day long he was singing, whistling, yelling, whooping, laughing—it was maddening, devastating, unendurable. At last, one day, I lost all my temper and went raging to my mother and said Sandy had been singing for an hour without a single break, and I couldn't stand it, and *wouldn't* she please shut him up. The tears came into her eyes and her lip trembled, and she said something like this:

"Poor thing, when he sings it shows that he is not remembering, and that comforts me; but when he is still I am afraid he is thinking and I cannot bear it. He will never see his mother again; if he can sing, I must not hinder it but be thankful for it. If you were older, you would understand me; then that friendless child's noise would make you glad."

It was a simple speech and made up of small words but it went home, and Sandy's noise was not a trouble to me any more. She never used large words but she had a natural gift for making small ones do effective work. She lived to reach the neighborhood of ninety years and was capable with her tongue to the last, especially when a meanness or an injustice roused her spirit. She has come handy to me several times in my books, where she figures as Tom Sawyer's Aunt Polly. I fitted her out with a dialect and tried to think up other improvements for her, but did not find any. I used Sandy once, also; it was in *Tom Sawyer*. I tried to get him to whitewash the fence but it did not work. I do not remember what name I called him by in the book.

I can see the farm yet with perfect clearness. I can see all its belongings, all its details: the family room of the house with a "trundle" bed in one corner and a spinning-wheel in another, a wheel whose rising and falling wail, heard from a distance, was the mournfulest of all sounds to me and made me homesick and low-spirited and filled my atmosphere with the wandering spirits of the dead; the vast fireplace, piled high on winter nights with flaming hickory logs from whose ends a sugary sap bubbled out but did not go to waste, for we scraped it off and ate it; the lazy cat spread out on the rough hearth-stone; the drowsy dogs braced against the jambs and blinking; my aunt in one chimney corner, knitting; my uncle in the other, smoking his corn-cob pipe; the slick and carpetless oak floor faintly mirroring the dancing flame-tongues and freckled with black indentations where fire-coals had popped out and died a leisurely death; half a dozen children romping in the background twilight; split-bottomed chairs here and there, some with rockers; a cradle, out of service but waiting with confidence; in the early cold mornings a snuggle of children in shirts and chemises occupying the hearth-stone and procrastinating—they could not bear to leave that comfortable place and go out on the wind-swept floor-space between the house and kitchen where the general tin basin stood, and wash.

Along outside of the front fence ran the country road, dusty in the summertime and a good place for snakes—they liked to lie in it and sun themselves; when they were rattlesnakes or puff adders, we killed them; when they were black snakes or racers or belonged to the fabled "hoop" breed, we fled, without shame; when they were "house-snakes" or "garters" we carried them home and put them in Aunt Patsy's work-basket for a surprise; for she was prejudiced against snakes and always when she took the basket in her lap and they began to climb out of it, it disordered her mind. She never could seem to get used to them, her opportunities went for nothing. And she was always cold toward bats, too, and could not bear them; and yet I think a bat is as friendly a bird as there is. My mother was Aunt Patsy's sister and had the same wild superstitions. A bat is beautifully soft and silky; I do not know any creature that is pleasanter to the touch or is more grateful for caressings, if offered in the right spirit. I know all about these coleoptera because our great cave, three miles below Hannibal, was multitudinously stocked with them and often I brought them home to amuse my mother with. It was easy to manage if it was a school day, because then I had ostensibly been to school and hadn't any bats. She was not a suspicious person but full of trust and confidence, and when I said, "There's something in my coat-pocket for you," she would put her hand in. But she always took it out again, herself; I didn't have to tell her. It was remarkable, the way she couldn't learn to like private bats. The more experience she had, the more she could not change her views.

I think she was never in the cave in her life; but everybody else went there. Many excursion parties came from considerable distances up and down the river to visit the cave. It was miles in extent and was a tangled wilderness of narrow and lofty clefts and passages. It was an easy place to get lost in; anybody could do it, including the bats. I got lost in it myself, along with a lady, and our last candle burned down to almost nothing before we glimpsed the search party's lights winding about in the distance.

"Injun Joe," the half-breed, got lost in there once and would have starved to death if the bats had run short. But there was no chance of that, there were myriads of them. He told me all his story. In the book called *Tom Sawyer* I starved him entirely to death in the cave but that was in the interest of art; it never happened. "General" Gaines, who was our first town drunkard before Jimmy Finn got the place, was lost in there for the space of a week and finally pushed his handkerchief out of a hole in a hilltop near Saverton, several miles down the river from the cave's mouth, and somebody saw it and dug him out. There is nothing the matter with his statistics except the handkerchief. I knew him for years and he hadn't any. But it could have been his nose. That would attract attention.

The cave was an uncanny place for it contained a corpse, the corpse of a young girl of fourteen. It was in a glass cylinder inclosed in a copper one which was suspended from a rail which bridged a narrow passage. The body was preserved in alcohol, and it was said that loafers and rowdies used to drag it up by the hair and look at the dead face. The girl was the daughter of a St. Louis surgeon of extraordinary ability and wide celebrity. He was an eccentric man and did many strange things. He put the poor thing in that forlorn place himself.

Beyond the road where the snakes sunned themselves was a dense young thicket, and through it a dim-lighted path led a quarter of a mile; then out of the dimness one emerged abruptly upon a level great prairie which was covered with wild strawberry plants, vividly starred with prairie pinks, and walled in on all sides by forests. The strawberries were fragrant and fine and in the season we were generally there in the crisp freshness of the early morning, while the dew-beads still sparkled upon the grass and the woods were ringing with the first songs of the birds.

Down the forest slopes to the left were the swings. They were made of bark stripped from hickory saplings. When they became dry they were dangerous. They usually broke when a child was forty feet in the air, and this was why so many bones had to be mended every year. I had no ill luck myself, but none of my cousins escaped. There were eight of them and at one time and another they broke fourteen arms among them. But it cost next to nothing, for the doctor worked by the year—twenty-five dollars for the whole family. I remember two of the Florida doctors, Chowning and Meredith. They not only tended an entire family for twenty-five dollars a year but furnished the medicines themselves. Good measure, too. Only the largest persons could hold a whole dose. Castor oil was the principal beverage. The dose was half a dipperful, with half a dipperful of New Orleans molasses added to help it down and make it taste good, which it never did. The next standby was calomel, the next rhubarb, and the next jalap. Then they bled the patient and put mustard plasters on him. It was a dreadful system and yet the death rate was not heavy. The calomel was nearly sure to salivate the patient and cost him some of his teeth. There were no dentists. When teeth became touched with decay or were otherwise ailing, the doctor knew of but one thing to do: he fetched his tongs and dragged them out. If the jaw remained, it was not his fault. Doctors were not called in cases of ordinary illness; the family grandmother attended to those. Every old woman was a doctor and gathered her own medicines in the woods, and knew how to compound doses that would stir the vitals of a cast-iron dog. And then there was the "Indian doctor," a grave savage, remnant of his tribe, deeply read in the mysteries of nature and the secret properties of herbs; and most backwoodsmen had high faith in his powers and could tell of wonderful cures achieved by him. In Mauritius, away off yonder in the solitudes of the Indian Ocean, there is a person who answers to our Indian doctor of the old times. He is a Negro and has had no teaching as a doctor, yet there is one disease which he is master of and can cure and the doctors can't. They send for him when they have a case. It is a child's disease of a strange and deadly sort, and the Negro cures it with an herb medicine which he makes himself, from a prescription which has come down to him from his father and grandfather. He will not let anyone see it. He keeps the secret of its components to himself, and it is feared that he will die without divulging it; then there will be consternation in Mauritius. I was told these things by the people there, in 1896.

We had the "faith doctor" too, in those early days, a woman. Her specialty was toothache. She was a farmer's old wife and lived five miles from Hannibal. She would lay her hand on the patient's jaw and say, "Believe!" and the cure was prompt. Mrs. Utterback. I remember her very well. Twice I rode out there behind my mother, horseback, and saw the cure performed. My mother was the patient.

Dr. Meredith removed to Hannibal by and by, and was our family physician there, and saved my life several times. Still, he was a good man and meant well. Let it go.

I was always told that I was a sickly and precarious and tiresome and uncertain child, and lived mainly on allopathic medicines during the first seven years of my life. I asked my mother about this in her old age—she was in her eighty-eighth year—and said:

"I suppose that during all that time you were uneasy about me?"

"Yes, the whole time."

"Afraid I wouldn't live?"

After a reflective pause, ostensibly to think out the facts, "No—afraid you would."

The country school-house was three miles from my uncle's farm. It stood in a clearing in the woods and would hold about twenty-five boys and girls. We attended the school with more or less regularity once or twice a week in summer, walking to it in the cool of the morning by the forest paths and back in the gloaming at the end of the day. All the pupils brought their dinners in baskets—corn dodger, buttermilk, and other good things— and sat in the shade of the trees at noon and ate them. It is the part of my education which I look back upon with the most satisfaction. My first visit to the school was when I was seven. A strapping girl of fifteen, in the customary sunbonnet and calico dress, asked me if I "used tobacco," meaning did I chew it. I said no. It roused her scorn. She reported me to all the crowd, and said:

"Here is a boy seven years old who can't chew tobacco."

By the looks and comments which this produced I realized that I was a degraded object, and was cruelly ashamed of myself. I determined to reform. But I only made myself sick; I was not able to learn to chew tobacco. I learned to smoke fairly well but that did not conciliate anybody and I remained a poor thing, and characterless. I longed to be respected but I never was able to rise. Children have but little charity for each other's defects.

As I have said, I spent some part of every year at the farm until I was twelve or thirteen years old. The life which I led there with my cousins was full of charm and so is the memory of it yet. I can call back the solemn twilight and mystery of the deep woods, the earthy smells, the faint odors of the wild flowers, the sheen of rain-washed foliage, the rattling clatter of drops when the wind shook the trees, the far-off hammering of wood-peckers and the muffled drumming of wood-pheasants in the remoteness of the forest, the snapshot glimpses of disturbed wild creatures scurrying through the grass—I can call it all back and make it as real as it ever was, and as blessed. I can call back the prairie, and its loneliness and peace, and a vast hawk hanging motionless in the sky with his wings spread wide and the blue of the vault showing through the fringe of their end-feathers. I can see the woods in their autumn dress, the oak purple, the hickories washed with gold, the maples and the sumachs luminous with crimson fires, and I can hear the rustle made by the fallen leaves as we plowed through them. I can see the blue clusters of wild grapes hanging amongst the foliage of the saplings, and I remember the taste of them and the smell. I know how the wild blackberries looked and how they tasted; and the same with the pawpaws, the hazelnuts, and the persimmons; and I can feel the thumping rain upon my head of hickory-nuts and walnuts when we were out in the frosty dawn to scramble for them with the pigs, and the gusts of wind loosed them and sent them down. I know the stain of blackberries and how pretty it is, and I know the stain of walnut hulls and how little it minds soap and water, also what grudged experience it had of either of them. I know the taste of maple sap and when to gather it, and how to arrange the troughs and the delivery tubes, and how to boil down the juice, and how to hook the sugar after it is made; also how much better hooked sugar tastes than any that is honestly come by, let bigots say what they will.

I know how a prize watermelon looks when it is sunning its fat rotundity among pumpkin vines and "simblins"; I know how to tell when it is ripe without "plugging" it. I know how inviting it looks when it is cooling itself in a tub of water under the bed, waiting; I know how it looks when it lies on the table in the sheltered great floor-space between house and kitchen, and the children gathered for the sacrifice and their mouths watering. I know the crackling sound it makes when the carving knife enters its end and I can see the split fly along in front of the blade as the knife cleaves its way to the other end; I can see its halves fall apart and display the rich red meat and the black seeds, and the heart standing up, a luxury fit for the elect. I know how a boy looks behind a yard-long slice of that melon and I know how he feels, for I have been there. I know the taste of the watermelon which has been honestly come by and I know the taste of the watermelon which has been acquired by art. Both taste good but the experienced know which tastes best.

I know the look of green apples and peaches and pears on the trees, and I know how entertaining they are when they are inside of a person. I know how ripe ones look when they are piled in pyramids under the trees, and how pretty they are and how vivid their colors. I know how a frozen apple looks in a barrel down-cellar in the wintertime, and how hard it is to bite and how the frost makes the teeth ache, and yet how good it is notwithstanding. I know the disposition of elderly people to select the speckled apples for the children and I once knew ways to beat the game. I know the look of an apple that is roasting and sizzling on a hearth on a winter's evening, and I know the comfort that comes of eating it hot, along with some sugar and a drench of cream. I know the delicate art and mystery of so cracking hickory-nuts and walnuts on a flatiron with a hammer that the kernels will be delivered whole, and I know how the nuts, taken in conjunction with winter apples, cider, and doughnuts, make old people's old tales and old jokes sound fresh and crisp and enchanting, and juggle an evening away before you know what went with the time. I know the look of Uncle Dan'l's kitchen as it was on privileged nights when I was a child, and I can see the white and black children grouped on the hearth, with the firelight playing on their faces and the shadows flickering upon the walls clear back toward the cavernous gloom of the rear, and I can hear Uncle Dan'l telling the immortal tales which Uncle Remus Harris was to gather into his book and charm the world with, by and by. And I can feel again the creepy joy which quivered through me when the time for the ghost story was reached—and the sense of regret too which came over me, for it was always the last story of the evening and there was nothing between it and the unwelcome bed.

Carl Van Doren was born in Hope, Illinois, and educated at the University of Illinois and at Columbia University, where he completed a Ph.D. in 1911, at which time he also published his first novel. From 1911 to 1930 he taught English at Columbia, completed another novel, The Ninth Wave, and wrote many critical essays on American writers and their works. Some of his best-known books are Contemporary American Novelists, The Roving Critic, and Many Minds. He has also edited The Cambridge History of American Literature (1921) and American and British Literature (1925). He was awarded the Pulitzer Prize for his biography of Benjamin Franklin.

(1885-1950)

CARL VAN DOREN

Van Doren's tightly structured "A Note on the Essay" illustrates the scholarship and clarity that characterize his work as editor and literary critic.

A Note on the Essay

The sonnet has a standard form very much as a man has. Leave off the sestet of your sonnet and you do about what a God does when he leaves the legs off a man. The drama has a standard form very much as a rendezvous has. Write a drama in which no spark is exchanged between the audience and the action, and you have done what fate does when it keeps lovers from their meeting. The novel has a standard form very much as a road has. You may set out anywhere you like and go wherever you please, at any gait, but you must go somewhere, or you have made what is no more a novel than some engineer's road would be a road if it had neither beginning, end, nor direction. But the essay! It may be of any length, breadth, depth, weight, density, color, savor, odor, appearance, importance, value, or uselessness which you can or will give it. The epigram bounds it on one side and the treatise on the other, but it has in its time encroached upon the territory of both of them, and it doubtless will do so again. Or, to look at the essay from another angle, it is bounded on one side by the hell-fire sermon and on the other by the geometric demonstration; and yet it ranges easily between these extremes of heat and cold and occasionally steals from both of them. It differs from a letter by being written to more—happily a great many more—than one person. It differs from talk chiefly by being written at all.

Having to obey no regulations as to form, the essay is very free to choose its matter. The sonnet, by reason of its form, tends to deal with solemn and not with gay themes. The drama, for the same reason, tends to look for intense and not for casual incidents. The novel tends to feel that it must carry a considerable amount of human life on its back. The essay may be as fastidious as a collector of carved emeralds or as open-minded as a garbage-gatherer. Nothing human, as the platitude says, is alien to it. The essay, however, goes beyond the platitude and dares to choose matter from numerous non-human sources. Think of the naturalists and their essays. Think, further, of the range of topics for essayists at large. Theodore Roosevelt in an essay urges the strenuous life; Max Beerbohm in an essay defends cosmetics. DeQuincey expounds the fine art of murder, Thoreau the pleasures of economy, William Law the blisses of prayer, Hudson the sense of smell in men and in animals, Schopenhauer the ugliness of women, Bacon the advantages of a garden, Plutarch the traits of curiosity, and A C. Benson the felicity of having nothing much in the mind. All, in fact, an essayist needs to start with is something, anything, to say. He gets up each morning and finds the world spread out before him, as the world was spread out before Adam and Eve the day they left paradise. With the cosmos, past, present, and future, to pick from, the essayist goes to work. If he finds a topic good enough he may write a good essay, no matter how he writes it.

He may. There is still, however, the question of his manner. Thousands of dull men have written millions of true things which no one but their proofreaders, wives, or pupils ever read. If each essayist could take out a patent on each subject into which he dips his pen, and could prevent any other pen from ever dipping into it after him, he might have better luck. But there are no monopolists in this department. Would research find in all the hoards of books or all the morgues of manuscripts a single observation which has never been made twice? Competition in such affairs is free and endless. The only law which gives an essayist a right to his material is the law which rules that the best man wins. The law does not say in what fashion he must be best. Any fashion will do. Let him be more sententious, like Bacon; or more harmonious, like Sir Thomas Browne; or more elegant, like Addison; or more direct, like Swift; or more hearty, like Fielding; or more whimsical, like Lamb; or more impassioned, like Hazlitt; or more encouraging, like Emerson; or more Olympian, like Arnold; or more funny, like Mark Twain; or more musical, like Pater; or more impish, like Max Beerbohm; or more devastating, like Mencken. Let the essayist be any of these things and he may have a copyright till someone takes it away from him. What matters is the manner. If he has good matter, he *may* write a good essay; if he has a good manner he probably *will* write a good essay.

An essay is a communication. If the subject of the discourse were the whole affair, it would be enough for the essayist to be an adequate conduit. If the manner were the whole affair, any versatile fellow might try all the manners and have a universal triumph. But back of matter and manner both lies the item which is really significant. The person who communicates anything in any way must be a person. His truth must have a tone, his speech must have a rhythm, which are his and solely his.   His knowledge or opinions must have lain long enough inside him to have taken root there; and when they come away they must bring some of the soil clinging to them.   They must, too, have been shaped by that soil—as plants are which grow in cellars, on housetops, on hillsides, in the wide fields, under shade in forests.   Many kinds of men, many kinds of essays!   Important essays come from important men.

— reprinted from <u>The New Pearsons</u>*; with permission of the estate of Carl Van Doren*

Gilbert Keith Chesterton was born in London and educated at St. Paul's school, where he soon revealed his ability to write—even though he had an undistinguished record in other subjects.

After a few years as reviewer, journalist, and writer for The Bookman *and other British publications, Chesterton turned to free-lance work. He produced a great variety of essays, poems, biographies, plays, novels, and short stories. His "Father Brown" stories, in which a priest-detective is always able to get his man, have been very popular.*

Chesterton was witty, kindly, and humanitarian. Although he had a short rebellious period, he was inclined to be conservative, and in his essays frequently argued for traditional beliefs and practices, and against innovations. His nimble wit and his ability to use metaphor, analogy, and paradox enabled him to defend his position in any argument. In the following essay, Chesterton points out that our emphasis upon efficiency and deadlines should not be permitted to destroy all individual freedom.

(*1874-1936*)

G. K. CHESTERTON

On Lying in Bed

Lying in bed would be an altogether perfect and supreme experience if only one had a coloured pencil long enough to draw on the ceiling. This, however, is not generally a part of the domestic apparatus on the premises. I think myself that the thing might be managed with several pails of Aspinall and a broom. Only if one worked in a really sweeping and masterly way, and laid on the colour in great washes, it might drip down again on one's face in floods of rich and mingled colour like some strange fairy rain; and that would have its disadvantages. I am afraid it would be necessary to stick to black and white in this form of artistic composition. To that purpose, indeed, the white ceiling would be of the greatest possible use; in fact, it is the only use I think of a white ceiling being put to.

But for the beautiful experiment of lying in bed I might never have discovered it. For years I have been looking for some blank spaces in a modern house to draw on. Paper is much too small for any really allegorical design; as Cyrano de Bergerac says: "*Il me faut des géants.*" But when I tried to find these fine clear spaces in the modern rooms such as we all live in I was continually disappointed. I found an endless pattern and complication of small objects hung like a curtain of fine links between me and my desire. I examined the walls; I found them to my surprise to be already covered with wall-paper, and I found the wall-paper to be already covered with very uninteresting images, all bearing a ridiculous resemblance to each other. I could not understand why one arbitrary symbol (a symbol apparently entirely devoid of any religious or philosophical significance) should thus be sprinkled all over my nice walls like a sort of small-pox. The Bible must be referring to wall-papers, I think, when it says, "Use not vain repetitions, as the Gentiles do." I found the Turkey carpet a mass of unmeaning colours, rather like the Turkish Empire, or like the sweetmeat called Turkish Delight. I do not exactly know what Turkish Delight really is; but I suppose it is Macedonian Massacres. Everywhere that I went forlornly, with my pencil or my paint brush, I found that others had unaccountably been before me, spoiling the walls, the curtains, and the furniture with their childish and barbaric designs.

*   *   *

Nowhere did I find a really clear space for sketching until this occasion when I prolonged beyond the proper limit the process of lying on my back in bed. Then the light of that white heaven broke upon my vision, that breadth of mere white which is indeed almost the definition of Paradise, since it means purity and also means freedom. But alas! like all heavens now that it is seen it is found to be unattainable; it looks more austere and more distant than the blue sky outside the window. For my proposal to paint on it with the bristly end of a broom has been discouraged—never mind by whom, by a person debarred from all political rights—and even my minor proposal to put the other end of the broom into the kitchen fire and turn it into charcoal has not been conceded. Yet I am certain that it was from persons in my position that all the original inspiration came for covering the ceilings of palaces and cathedrals with a riot of fallen angels or victorious gods. I am sure that it was only because Michael Angelo was engaged in the ancient and honourable occupation of lying in bed that he ever realized how the roof of the Sistine Chapel might be made into an awful imitation of a divine drama that could only be acted in the heavens.

The tone now commonly taken towards the practice of lying in bed is hypocritical and unhealthy. Of all the marks of modernity that seem to mean a kind of decadence, there is none more menacing and dangerous than the exaltation of very small and secondary matters of conduct at the expense of very great and primary ones, at the expense of eternal ties and tragic human morality. If there is one thing worse than the modern weakening of major morals it is the modern strengthening of minor morals. Thus it is considered more withering to accuse a man of bad taste than of bad ethics. Cleanliness is not next to godliness nowadays, for cleanliness is made an essential and godliness is regarded as an offence. A playwright can attack the institution of marriage so long as he does not misrepresent the manners of society, and I have met Ibsenite pessimists who thought it wrong to take beer but right to take prussic acid. Especially is this so in matters of hygiene; notably such matters as lying in bed. Instead of being regarded, as it ought to be, as a matter of personal convenience and adjustment, it has come to be regarded by many as if it were a part of essential morals to get up early in the morning. It is, upon the whole, part of practical wisdom; but there is nothing good about it or bad about its opposite.

*　　*　　*

Misers get up early in the morning; and burglars, I am informed, get up the night before. It is the great peril of our society that all its mechanism may grow more fixed while its spirit grows more fickle. A man's minor actions and arrangements ought to be free, flexible, creative; the things that should be unchangeable are his principles, his ideals. But with us the reverse is true; our views change constantly; but our lunch does not change. Now, I should like men to have strong and rooted conceptions, but as for their lunch, let them have it sometimes in the garden, sometimes in bed, sometimes on the roof, sometimes in the top of a tree. Let them argue from the same first principles, but let them do it in a bed, or a boat, or a balloon. This alarming growth of good habits really means a too great emphasis on those virtues which mere custom can ensure; it means too little emphasis on those virtues which custom can never quite ensure, sudden and splendid virtues of inspired pity or of inspired candour. If ever that abrupt appeal is made to us we may fail. A man can get used to getting up at five o'clock in the morning. A man cannot very well get used to being burnt for his opinions; the first experiment is commonly fatal. Let us pay a little more attention to these possibilities of the heroic and the unexpected. I dare say that when I get out of this bed I shall do some deed of an almost terrible virtue.

For those who study the great art of lying in bed there is one emphatic caution to be added. Even for those who can do their work in bed (like journalists), still more for those whose work cannot be done in bed (as, for example, the professional harpooners of whales), it is obvious that the indulgence must be very occasional. But that is not the caution I mean. The caution is this: if you do lie in bed, be sure you do it without any reason or justification at all. I do not speak, of course, of the seriously sick. But if a healthy man lies in bed, let him do it without a rag of excuse; then he will get up a healthy man. It he does it for some secondary hygienic reason, if he has some scientific explanation, he may get up a hypochondriac.

— *reprinted with permission of Miss D. E. Collins from G. K. Chesterton's Tremendous Trifles (London, Methuen, 1909)*

Joseph Hilaire Belloc was born in France. His father was a French lawyer and his mother was the granddaughter of Joseph Priestley, the famous English scientist. After graduating from Oxford, he was elected to Parliament and served on the editorial staff of the Morning Post.

His writings vary from light verse to serious biographical studies. His books include The Bad Child's Book of Beasts, More Beasts for Worse Children; collections of essays entitled On Nothing, On Anything, and On Everything; and biographies of Robespierre, Danton, Cardinal Richelieu, and Cardinal Wolsey.

(1870-1953)

HILAIRE BELLOC

On Poverty

I had occasion the other day to give an address to a number of young men upon the matter of Poverty: which address I had intended to call "Poverty: The Attainment of It: the Retention of It when Attained." But I found that no explanation of my title was necessary. The young men knew all about it.

In giving this short address I discovered, as one always does in the course of speaking without notes, all manner of new aspects in the thing. The simple straightforward view of poverty we all know; how it is beneficial to the soul, what a training it is, how acceptable to the Higher Powers, and so on. We also know how all those men whom we are taught to admire began with poverty, and we all have, I hope, at the back of our minds a conception of poverty as a sort of foundation for virtue and right living.

But these ideas are general and vague. I was led by my discourse to consider the thing in detail, and to think out by reminiscence and reason certain small, solid, particular advantages in poverty, and also a sort of theory of maintenance in poverty: rules for remaining poor.

I thus discovered first of all a definition of poverty, which is this: Poverty is that state in which a man is perpetually anxious for the future of himself and his dependents, unable to pursue life upon a standard to which he was brought up, tempted both to subservience and to a sour revolt, and tending inexorably towards despair.

Such was the definition of poverty to which I arrived, and once arrived at, the good effects flowing from such a condition are very plain.

The first great good attendant upon poverty is that it makes men generous. You will notice that while some few of the rich are avaricious or mean, and while all of them have to be, from the very nature of their position, careful, the poor and embarrassed man will easily share whatever little he has. True, this is from no good motive, but merely from a conviction that, whatever he does, it will be much the same in the end; so that his kindness to his fellows comes from a mixture of weakness and indifference. Still, it breeds a habit; and that is why men whose whole characters have been formed under this kind of poverty always throw away money when by any chance they get a lump of it.

Then there is this other good attending poverty, that it cures one of illusions. The most irritating thing in the company of the rich, and especially of rich women, is the very morass of illusion in which they live. Indeed, it cannot be all illusion, there must be a good deal of conscious falsehood about it. But, at any rate, it is an abyss of unreality, communion with which at last becomes intolerable. Now the poor man is physically prevented from falling into such vices of the heart and intelligence. He cannot possibly think that the police are heroes, the judges superhuman beings, the motives of public men in general other than vile. He can nourish no fantasies upon the kind old family servant, or the captain of industry's supreme intelligence. The poor man is up against it, as the phrase goes. He is up against the bullying and corruption of the police, the inhuman stupidity of the captain of industry, the sly self-advancement of the lawyer, the abominable hypocrisies of the parasitical trades: such as buttling. He comes across all these things by contact and the direct personal sensible experience. He can no more think of mankind as a garden than a soldier can think of war as a picture, or a sailor of the sea as a pleasure-place.

We may also thank poverty (those of us who are enjoying her favours) for cutting quite out of our lives certain extraordinary necessities which haunt our richer brethren. I know a rich man who is under compulsion to change his clothes at least twice a day, and often thrice, to travel at set periods to set places, and to see in rotation each of at least sixty people. He has less freedom than a schoolboy in school, or a corporal in a regiment; indeed, he has no real leisure at all, because so many things are thus necessary to him. But your poor man cannot even conceive what these necessities may be. If you were to tell him that he *had* to go and soak himself in the vulgarity of the Riviera for so many weeks, he would not understand the word "had" at all. He would say that perhaps there were some people who liked that kind of thing, but that anyone should do it without a strongly perverted appetite he could not understand.

And here's another boon of grinding, anxious, sordid poverty. There is no greater enemy of the soul than sloth; but in this state of ceaseless dull exasperation, like a kind of grumbling toothache, sloth is impossible. Yet another enemy of the soul is pride, and even the sour poor man cannot really nourish pride; he may wish to nourish it; he may hope in future to nourish it; but he cannot immediately nourish it. Or, again, the inmost of man which an old superstition called "the Soul" is hurt by luxury. Now poverty, in the long run, forbids or restricts luxury.

I know very well you will tell me with countless instances how the poor gentlemen of your acquaintance drink cocktails, eat caviare, go to the theatre (and that in the stalls), take taxis, order liqueurs with their coffee, and blow cheques. Very true, but if you will narrowly watch the careers of such, you will find that there is a progressive decline in these habits of theirs. The taxis get rarer and rarer after forty-five; caviare dies out; and though liqueur with coffee goes on, there is discipline, incredible as it may seem, imposed upon luxury by poverty. Indeed, I met a man only last April in a town called Lillebonne (where I was examining the effects of Roman remains upon hotel-keeping), and this man told me that before the War he habitually spent his holiday (he was a parson) in Switzerland, but now he could not get beyond Normandy. Whereupon I sketched for him on a piece of paper a scheme showing, with a radius vector (the same graduated, which, indeed, was my parson, also) and drawn to scale, the expenses of a holiday. Therein did I show him that a holiday killing lions in East Africa cost so much, another badgering the French in Morocco so much, another annoying the Spaniards so much: and how the cheapest holiday of all was a holiday on foot in Normandy, which lies but one poor Bradbury from the coasts of these islands. This little diagram he folded and took away—little knowing that a still cheaper holiday could be taken in the Ardennes.

Poverty, I think, however, has a much nobler effect by the introduction of irony, which I take to be the salt in the feast of intelligence. I have, indeed, known rich men to possess irony native to themselves, so that it is like a picture which a man paints for his own pleasure and puts up on his own walls. All the poor of London have irony, and, indeed, poor men all over the world have irony; even poor gentlemen, after the age of fifty, discover veins of irony and are the better for them, as a man is better for sherry in his soup. Remark that irony kills stupid satire, and that to have an agent within one that kills stupid satire is to possess an antiseptic against the suppurative reactions of the mind.

Poverty, again, makes men appreciate reality. You may tell me that this is of no advantage. It is of no direct advantage, but I am sure it is of advantage in the long run, for if you ignore reality you will come sooner or later against it, like a ship against a rock in a fog, and you will suffer as the ship will suffer.

If you say to the rich man that some colleague of his has genius, he may admit it in a lazy but sincere fashion. A poor man knows better; he may admit it with his lips, but he is not so foolish as to accept it.

Lastly, of poverty, I think this, that it prepares one very carefully for the grave. I heard it said once by a beggar in a passion that the rich took nothing with them down to death. In the literal acceptation of the text he was wrong, for the rich take down with them to death flattery, folly, illusion, pride, and a good many other lesser garments which have grown into their skins, and the tearing off of which at the great stripping must hurt a good deal. But I know what this mendicant meant—he meant that they take nothing with them down to the grave in the way of motor-cars, hot water, clean change of clothes, and various intolerably boring games. The rich go down to death stripped of external things not grown into their skins; the poor go down to death stripped of everything. Therefore in Charon's boat they get forward, and are the first upon the further shore. And this, I suppose, is some sort of advantage.

— reprinted by permission of A. D. Peters & Co.; from Hilaire Belloc's <u>A Conversation with an Angel</u> *(London, Jonathan Cape, 1928)*

Dreiser was born in Terre Haute, Indiana. His formal education ended with one year (1888-1889) at Indiana University.

In his early years Dreiser felt the impact of poverty, and his disheartening early experiences gave him a lifelong sympathy for the underdog. He worked as a journalist and editor while the publication of his first novel was being blocked by censorship, of a kind that tended to increase his dislike for puritanism and bourgeois hypocrisy.

Dreiser belonged to the "naturalist" group of writers who believed that the writer's task was to place his characters in a certain situation and then observe and report the results, just as a scientist conducts and reports an experiment in biology or the physical sciences. His chief works include Sister Carrie (1900), The Financier (1912), The Genius (1915), and An American Tragedy (1925). Sister Carrie was condemned by numerous critics because of its extreme frankness. The Financier dealt with "big business," and An American Tragedy attempts to assess the causes that led a young man to commit a murder.

(1871-1945)

THEODORE DREISER

On Being Poor

Poverty is so relative. I have lived to be thirty-two now, and am just beginning to find that out. Hitherto, in no vague way, poverty to me seemed to be indivisibly united with the lack of money. And this in the face of a long series of experiences which should have proved to any sane person that this was only relatively true. Without money, or at times with so little that an ordinary day laborer would have scoffed at my supply, I still found myself meditating gloomily and with much show of reason upon the poverty of others. But what I was really complaining of, if I had only known, was not poverty of material equipment (many of those whom I pitied were materially as well if not better supplied than I was) but poverty of mind, the most dreadful and inhibiting and destroying of all forms of poverty. There are others, of course: Poverty of strength, of courage, of skill. And in respect to no one of these have I been rich, but poverty of mind, of the understanding, of taste, of imagination—therein lies the true misery, the freezing degradation of life.

For I walk through the streets of this great city—so many of them no better than the one in which I live—and see thousands upon thousands,

— reprinted by arrangement with The World Publishing Co. from Theodore Dreiser's The Color of a Great City; © 1923 by Boni and Liveright, Inc.; © 1951 by Helen R. Dreiser

materially no worse off than myself, many of them much better placed, yet with whom I would not change places save under conditions that could not be met, the principal one being that I be permitted to keep my own mind, my own point of view. For here comes one whose clothes are good but tasteless or dirty; and I would not have his taste or his dirt. And here is another whose shabby quarters cost him as much as do mine and more, and yet I would not live in the region which he chooses for half his rent, nor have his mistaken notion of what is order, beauty, comfort. Nothing short of force could compel me. And here is one sufficiently well dressed and housed, as well dressed and housed as myself, who still consorts with friends from whom I could take no comfort, creatures of so poor a mentality that it would be torture to associate with them.

And yet how truly poor, materially, I really am. For over a year now the chamber in which I dwell has cost me no more than four dollars a week. My clothes, with the exception of such minor changes as ties and linen, are the very same I have had for several years. I am so poor at this writing that I have not patronized a theatre in months. A tasteful restaurant such as always I would prefer has this long while been beyond my purse. I have even been beset by a nervous depression which has all but destroyed my power to write, or to sell that which I might write. And, as I well know, illness and death might at any time interfere and cut short the struggle that in my case has thus far proved materially most profitless; and yet, believe me, I have never felt poor, or that I have been cheated of much that life might give. Nor have I felt that sense of poverty that appears to afflict thousands of those about me.

I cannot go to a theatre, for instance, lacking the means. But I can and do go to many of the many, many museums, exhibits, collections, and arboreta that are open to me for nothing in this great city. And for greater recreation even, I turn to such books of travel, of discovery, of scientific and philosophic investigation and speculation as chance to fit in with my mood at the time and with which a widespread public beneficence has provided me, and where I find such pleasure, such relief, such delights as I should hesitate to attempt to express in words.

But apart from these, which are after all but reports of and commentaries upon the other, comes the beauty of life itself. I know it to be a shifting, lovely, changeful thing ever, and to it, the spectacle of it as a whole, in my hours of confusion and uncertainty I invariably return, and find such marvels of charm in color, tone, movement, arrangement, which, had I the genius to report, would fill the museums and the libraries of the world to overflowing with its masterpieces. The furies of snow and rain that speed athwart a hidden sun. The wracks and wisps of cloud that drape a winter or a summer moon. A distant, graceful tower from which a flock of pigeons soar. The tortuous, tideful rivers that twist among great forests of masts and under many graceful bridges. The crowding, surging ways of seeking men. These cost me nothing, and I weary of them never.

And sunsets. And sunrises. And moonsets. And moonrises. These are not things to which those materially deficient would in the main turn for solace, but to me they are substances of solace, the major portion of all my wealth or possible wealth, in exchange for which I would not take a miser's hoard. I truly would not.

At the age of twenty-four, Irwin Edman graduated with a Ph.D. from Columbia and then joined the staff of that university as a lecturer in the Department of Philosophy. Though he was associated with Columbia for the rest of his life, Edman was frequently a guest lecturer at other universities and colleges, including Harvard, the University of California, Amherst College, and the University of Brazil. A rather dishevelled little man with an amazing memory and a brilliant mind, he gained a reputation as a stimulating teacher whose classes were always large and well attended.

Edman published a volume of poems in 1925. In addition, he wrote a number of books, including Four Ways of Philosophy (1937), Philosopher's Holiday (1938), Art and the Man (1939), Philosopher's Quest (1947), and Under Whatever Sky (1951). He also contributed numerous articles to The Nation, The New Republic, the New York Times, Harper's, The Saturday Review of Literature, the Atlantic Monthly, and the New Yorker.

(1896-1954)

IRWIN EDMAN

Behind Edman's essay on American leisure is his knowledge of history, sociology, and philosophy. However, we note that these studies do not result in a series of abstractions; instead he presents a clear, well-organized assessment of American behavior.

On American Leisure

The best test of the quality of a civilization is the quality of its leisure. Not what the citizens of a commonwealth do when they are obliged to do something by necessity, but what they do when they can do anything by choice, is the criterion of a people's life. One can tell much about a man by noting the objects and pastimes to which he spontaneously turns for joy. The same may be said of a nation. It was a suggestive comment of Maxim Gorky's on visiting Coney Island, "What an unhappy people it must be that turns for happiness here." The most serious criticism leveled against American civilization is not that its work is standardized and its business engulfing, but that its pleasures are mechanical and its leisure slavish. It is not that we have not time. Foreign observers are repeatedly astonished at the number of hours an ever-increasing number of Americans have to themselves. It is not time we lack, but leisure.

Leisure is indeed an affair of mood and atmosphere rather than simply of the clock. It is not a chronological occurrence but a spiritual state. It is unhurried pleasurable living among one's native enthusiasms. Leisure consists of those pauses in our lives when experience is a fusion of stimulation and repose. Genuine leisure yields at once a feeling of vividness and sense of peace. It consists of moments so clear and pleasant in themselves that one might wish they were eternal.

For travelled Americans, at least, the best illustrations and memories of such experiences will come from abroad. For one it will be the recollection of keen but casual conversation at tea on a lawn in Sussex or Surrey. For another it will be the image of two friends chatting over coffee and liqueurs at an *al fresco* table on a boulevard in Paris. Another will remember a stroll in an Italian piazza or a long, dignified peace of an evening in a London club.

It is not that one cannot find domestic images, too, of a quality of leisure that seems to be passing almost completely out of the American scene. Many a middle-aged American, in the midst of a life crowded with social as well as business or professional obligations, will recall some rare hour that its golden and gratuitous irrelevance seems to belong not in the realm of time but in the careless length of eternity, an afternoon spent browsing without purpose in a library or walking without the thought of time or destination on the quiet windings of an unfrequented country road. One recalls conversations lightly begun after dinner and meandering through wreaths of smoke into unexpected depths and intensities until long after an unnoticed midnight. One remembers some incredibly remote year when one wrote by hand a letter that flowed on as if ink and paper and ideas would never end.

But for Americans the word "leisure" has distinctively Old World associations. That is partly because some Americans have there known it best. Cut off from the pressure and compulsions of their normal occupations at home, they have moved with freedom amid the grace of a leisurely tradition. But there is a deeper reason which lies in the contrast between that European tradition and our own. The quality of leisure in Europe is partly the heritage of a long leisure class tradition, partly the patience of peoples that have the sense of age and are not obsessed with hastening toward the new and building the possible in a hurry. In our own civilization, originally and in spirit partly pioneer, there is a working rather than a leisure class tradition, and the impress and atmosphere of work have come to control our lives even when we are not working. To be busy has been with us a primary virtue, and even our play has had to find a place for itself as a kind of business.

A number of years ago Professor Veblen in his *Theory of the Leisure Class* tried to point out how the traditions and interests of a leisure class had shaped our tastes and our morals. A quite plausible volume might be written on the thesis that the pursuit of leisure in our civilization is determined by our traditions of work; we carry the morals and ideals of an essentially industrial, essentially business civilization over into our play.

Leisure—a quiet and emancipated absorption in things and doings for their own sake—has always seemed to us effeminate and exotic. We wish leisure for relief, for release, for escape; for instruction, enlightenment, or advancement. There is something immoral about moments that are good in themselves. There is probably no other country in the world where idleness is one of the deadly sins.

With us, therefore, leisure has been a melodramatic escape into excitement, or a moralistic flight into self-improvement. We oscillate between night clubs and outlines of culture. Every one has at some time or other been present at a determinedly gay party. He has seen ordinarily quiet, intelligent people become wilfully noisy and stupid. He has seen men and women, separately delightful and entertaining, prance about loudly, screaming vulgarities, acting the "grown-up babies of the age." And his pain has been increased by a sense that none of these people cared to do the silly things they were doing. They drank more than they really wished to, and uttered hiccoughing nonsense that they themselves despised.

Every one, likewise, has listened to a group of people at dinner or afterwards, talk with obligatory boredom about the modish books and plays and ideas. Spontaneity, which is of the essence of any truly spiritual life, flies out of the conversation and out of the window, when "culture" becomes deliberate. We settle down as grimly to being serious as we settle down to being silly. Between the foolish and the funereal we have managed to find no middle course.

Of escapes from the pressure of an increasingly mechanized life to occasional outbursts of excitement or triviality there is much to be said. At least it may be said for them that they are natural, perhaps needful, refuges from a world whose tightly woven days would otherwise be unbearable. It is perhaps a sad commentary on the angular and constricted lives we lead that we should have to seek lurid and futile ways to peace. But it is not to be wondered at that, living in such a world of routine, we should plunge ever so often into the loud nonsense of inane parties, wallow in the absurd pathos and comedy of the screen, or fall enraptured victims to successive crazes of footless puzzles and dull games. We may be forgiven our excursions to musical comedies without wit or music, and conversational evenings without humanity or ideas. The contemporary citizen is vexed beyond his own realization by the humdrum unthrilling pressure of his days; he craves naturally now and then an opportunity to be trivial, irresponsible, and absurd.

But the irony of our situation lies in the fact that even when we try to escape into triviality or foolishness we make a serious and standardized business of it. One can pardon occasional madness in a sober civilization, but there is something pathetic, almost ghastly, in soberly making madness a routine. The half-drunken gayety that has become the accompaniment of much respectable social life is a sad determined business. Orgy has become a social obligation; dissipation a prescription to the weary, the repressed, and the disenchanted. It becomes as much a social obligation to play a new game or have a new thrill as to read a new book or wear a current collar or hat. Any number of "nice" people go systematically about becoming on occasion trivial, foolish, or mad. It is as if the American could not stop being efficient when he wanted to, and had to be gay or trivial or ecstatic with the same thoroughness and strained energy with which he might build a business or a skyscraper.

There are other reasons besides our own solemn efficiency that have been transforming our attempts to amuse ourselves into pale and standard routines. The same forces that have gone into the big business of providing our necessities have gone into the big business of providing our amusements. One may glamorously state the possibilities of the radio, the universalization of beautiful music and distinguished thought. One may talk as one will about the possible high art of the moving picture, marvel as one will at the new mechanical perfections of the phonograph. There is no question but that these are at their best mechanical. They turn our leisure into a passive receptivity of standard mediocre amusement. They provide almost nothing of that spontaneous sense of individual living which is part of the repose and stimulation of leisure. It is not pleasant to realize that our leisure is taking on the color—or colorlessness—of the rest of our lives; that we are becoming stereotypes in our play as in our work. The most serious spiritual danger of the Industrial Revolution is that it has come to mechanize and industrialize not merely things but the spirit as well.

When a man is at leisure we like to say he is free to be himself, but if his freedom consists in efficiently amusing himself according to the standard formulas or subjecting himself to the passive reception of standard amusements, he is not free at all.

But while leisure has in one direction gone toward conventional amusement and stereotyped triviality, in another direction it has become a kind of elegant overtime work. The latest use we have found for leisure is to make it useful. Its usefulness, which might have been supposed to be that it was a good in itself, has been transformed into its possibility as a means of systematic self-improvement. Correspondence courses, outlines of knowledge, scrapbooks of learning—agencies not always disinterested—have been trying to teach us what we might do with our unharnessed moments if only we would harness them. A little less carousal and a little less bridge, and we might become heirs to all of Western culture, or experts in philosophy or French. There is a revealing irrelevance in the reasons assigned for turning the casual moments of our lives to the pursuit of knowledge. It is not that knowledge will render us self-possessed and whole, that it will give wings to our imagination and give a larger, clearer, and sweeter horizon to our lives. It is that knowledge, or a smattering of it, will make us successful or respected, that a veneer of garbled French will reveal our breeding, or a parade of the names of philosophers testify to our intellectual curiosity. There is possibly no clearer index to the remoteness of a native American culture than the eager indiscriminate voracity with which Americans gobble up tabloid versions of fields of expert knowledge. Far from meaning that we have turned to the love of wisdom, it means that we have turned our idle hours into the hurried business of getting short cuts to knowledge. Outlines simply are a way of applying efficiency to culture as well as to business. Their very essence is to say that here is all philosophy or history or literature for those who have not the patience or sympathy to explore any corner of any of them with disinterested delight. Worst of all, they have taken from leisure its saving essence—the sense of doing some lovely thing for its own lovable sake.

There are aristocratic pessimists in our midst who hold that leisure in the sense of a fine spontaneous use of free time is increasingly impossible in America. They point to the facts cited in the foregoing and to other equally distressing social habits. The omnipresence of the automobile is not simply a temptation to literal speed, but has come to be a symbol for speed in spiritual matters as well. The only excitement in any activity, even in the pursuit of truth, is the excitement of going fast. It is for that reason, they insist, that there is no country where ideas become popular so fast as in America, no country where, half-learned, they are so quickly outmoded and forgotten. A book is the book of the month or at most a season, and the rapid-transit reader comes to forswear books for the reviews of them, and forswear reviews for excerpts from them in a synthetic magazine.

It is pointed out again, and with justice, that the multiplication of physical luxuries and physical distractions is a constant intruder upon that collectedness of spirit in which alone leisure can come to being. Serenity and integrity are menaced as much by the telephone as by any single invention of the last century. Long quiet waves of time have become almost impossible in evenings shattered by radios, by movies, and by the constant seduction and noise of the automobile. Speculation begins in a dreaming fantasy; meditation in reverie. In our contemporary urban world one almost never has a chance to achieve that half-drowsy detachment in which fantasy and reverie begin. We are kept too wide-awake ever to be really at peace or in thought. Finally, in a country where there is still a glamorous sense of unlimited opportunity, the desire for first place makes almost impossible that freedom and detachment which leave one free to follow an impulse for its own self-rewarding delight.

The desire for speed, the desire for luxury, the desire for first place— these are indeed three deadly enemies of leisure. In the current movement of American life there is not much prospect of radically overcoming them.

But there are portents of a change in our point of view that may portend a radical change in our practice.

There are growing evidences of a hunger for quiet and unhurried living among an increasing number of Americans. One cannot—nor would one—abolish the telephone or the automobile. There is no use in sighing for an anachronistic Paradise. It is impossible to transform life in New York in the twentieth century into the retirement of a rectory in Kent in the eighteenth. One cannot in the noise and hurry of a Western metropolitan winter pretend one is living in the timeless unconcern of an Eastern tropical island.

But part of our difficulty lies not in the impossibility of our circumstances, but in the blindness of our philosophy. If we once learned to rediscover the values of quiet spaces in our lives we should find a way to find them. There is time to be had even in New York or Chicago, and solitude even among crowds. One need not follow Thoreau into the wilderness to practise his isolation, nor Buddha into the desert to achieve his meditation. There is peace in a city apartment if one will but stay at home an evening to find it, and Nirvana to be found at home in one's own mind.

Ultimately the lack of leisure is lack of spiritual integration. We flee to society, dull though it be, through the fear of the greater dullness of being alone. We hurtle along at a breakneck speed, physically and spiritually, for fear of the drabness and futility we might feel if we slowed down. Any number of people are suddenly becoming aware of that situation and honest with themselves; are beginning to realize how much leisure one might have if one had enough faith in one's own resources. One need not let life be shattered into a splintered busyness by a routine absorption into social evenings which give one a standard good time. The rediscovery of solitude is being made by Americans, and with that rediscovery come many other delightful things: the chance to do nothing at all, not even talk, and the chance out of that interlude to follow a fancy or mediate a dream. Many a good citizen, given a chance to be alone with himself for an evening, might discover for the first time the quality of his own character, the contours of taste and interest that make him a personality as well as a jobholder and taxpayer. In such an interval a man may discover a hobby that will be for him a substitute for creative genius. He may not paint, write, or compose, but he may learn to do something indelibly himself and make something incredibly his own.

But in the golden days of leisure, in the spacious and graceful society of the Renaissance or the English country house, obviously men and women did not retire into their own souls away from the stimulation of other people. Good conversation is certainly one of the most enlivening ways of leisure, and good conversation is something between solemnity and absurdity. In America, of late, we have had to choose between talking on "subjects" solemnly and schematically, or babbling nonsense, doing anything rather than talk. We are, I think, beginning to learn again the joy of conversation, a light and easy play of minds and tempers over common human themes. We have grown a little weary of talk that is all smart and burnished; we have grown tired, too, of talk that sounds like the overflow program of a literary club. We are learning again that the meeting of minds and moods is one of the sweetest and most amiable fruits of human society. It has its own novelties and excitements no less than the automobile, radio, and bridge.

Not but that these last have their own special value as the pure gold of leisure. Even the mania for speed has about it something of the quality of poetry. No one who on some moonlight night has sped along a country road will deny the sheer poetical appeal that there is in the ease and freedom of speed. But the automobile has made the more peaceful kind of leisure possible as it never was before. It has brought the city dweller within easy reach of green and solitude. It has made neighbors of involuntary hermits. The radio, too, for all its blare of tawdry music, has put millions within the reach of formerly impossible musical beauty. It has brought Beethoven to the farmer and to apartment dwellers who could never be lured to Carneg.e Hall. And bridge, sniffed at by the cultured moralist, has its own justification. It is a diverting and harmless adventure of the mind and has for its devotees its own glories of wonder and conflict and surprise. If all these things are less interesting ultimately than conversation it is because we are social minds rather than aleatory machines.

There is, paradoxically enough, an incredible romanticism in our efficient impatience with leisure. We chase as madly as any early nineteenth-century German poet the Blue Flower of Happiness always beyond the hill. It is for that reason that we cannot take our idleness for the happiness it is; we try to turn it into an instrument toward the happiness it may bring. It may bring all knowledge into our province, or all salaries into our reach. It is for that reason that we have turned to outlines of knowledge and courses in success. But here, too, a change in spirit is notable.

There are men one knows who have made the surprised and delighted discovery that it is possible, if not to become hastily omniscient, at least to become patiently at home in some small field of knowledge or some tiny technic or art. It is not easy or particularly joyous to go into the whole vague history of mankind; but it is possible with pleasure to know one period or one decade of American history, or the story of one man or one movement. Only an octogenarian genius can master the whole of comparative literature; but any one can carve out a little pathway of poetry or prose, make one author, one genre, one theme his own, be it Trollope or sonnets, whaling or ballades. It is not possible for every man to be an artist; but almost any one can learn to draw or model, to play an instrument or plant a garden. In England one meets omniscient people no more than in America; nor are artists in every lane. But there are thousands of unpretentious lawyers or business men who have made some intimate little field of knowledge or thought their own, or learned to do one modest small hobby well.

We may talk much about the future of America, and think to measure its destiny by statistics of its educational, economic, or political changes. But the outlook for our country lies in the quality of its idleness almost as much as anything else.

Shall we then always alternate between trivial escapes into foolishness and solemn plunges into exploitation of our moments of repose? For us, as for Aristotle, there must be a golden mean. We may learn still to be at peace long enough to think and dream after our own fashion. We may learn to be together and be gay without being rowdy. We may learn to be expert in some little territory of art or thought or science without losing the amateur touch. We may still find time to live rather than time to kill.

If we do, we shall have learned what the spiritual life really means. For it means nothing more than those moments in experience when we have some free glint of life for its own sake, some lovely unforced glimmer of laughter or reason or love.

— reprinted from Irwin Edman's <u>Adam, the Baby, and the Man from Mars</u> (Houghton Mifflin Company, The Riverside Press, Cambridge, Mass., 1929); with permission of the publisher

A. G. Gardiner was born in Essex, England, and spent fifteen years on the staff of the Essex County Chronicle and the Northern Daily Telegraph before becoming editor of the London Daily News. Gardiner became known to many readers as "Alpha of the Plough," a pseudonym which he first used when contributing a series of essays to the London Star. Most of his essays and character sketches appeared in periodicals and in London newspapers. They were later published in several books, including Pebbles on the Shore (1916), Leaves in the Wind (1928), and Windfalls (1920).

The essay that follows indicates something of the mixture of perplexity and admiration with which a stranger in America (an English editor, for example) might watch a university football game with all its color and action. We note that he treats the game as an epic conflict, comparable to the ancient struggle between Greeks and Trojans. Students might decide for themselves whether his whole account is serious, whimsical, enthusiastic, or satirical.

(1865-1946)

ALFRED GEORGE GARDINER

Young America

"If you want to understand America," said my host, "come and see her young barbarians at play. Tomorrow Harvard meets Princeton at Princeton. It will be a great game. Come and see it."

He was a Harvard man himself, and spoke with the light of assured victory in his eyes. This was the first match since the war, but consider the record of the two Universities in the past. Harvard was as much ahead of Princeton on the football field as Oxford was ahead of Cambridge on the river. And I went to share his anticipated triumph. It was like a Derby Day at the Pennsylvania terminus at New York. From the great hall of that magnificent edifice a mighty throng of fur-coated men and women, wearing the favours of the rival colleges—yellow for Princeton and red for Harvard—passed through the gateways to the platform, filling train after train, that dipped under the Hudson and, coming out into the sunlight on the other side of the river, thundered away with its jolly load of revellers over the brown New Jersey country, through historic Trenton and on by woodland and farm to the far-off towers of Princeton.

And there, under the noble trees, and in the quads and the colleges, such a mob of men and women, young and old and middle-aged, such "how-d'ye-do's" and greetings, such meetings and recollections of old times and ancient matches, such hurrying and scurrying to see familiar haunts, class-room, library, chapel, refectories, everything treasured in the memory. Then off to the Stadium. There it rises like some terrific memorial of antiquity—

seen from without a mighty circular wall of masonry, sixty or seventy feet high; seen from within a great oval, or rather horseshoe, of humanity, rising tier above tier from the level of the playground to the top of the giddy wall. Forty thousand spectators—on this side of the horseshoe, the reds; on the other side, with the sunlight full upon them, the yellows.

Down between the rival hosts, and almost encircled by them, the empty playground, with its elaborate whitewash markings—for this American game is much more complicated than English Rugger—its goal-posts and its gigantic scoring boards that with their ten-foot letters keep up a minute record of the game.

The air hums with the buzz of forty thousand tongues. Through the buzz there crashes the sound of approaching music, martial music, challenging music, and the band of the Princeton men, with the undergrads marching like soldiers to the battlefield, emerges round the Princeton end of the horseshoe, and takes its place on the bottom rank of the Princeton host opposite. Terrific cheers from the enemy.

Another crash of music, and from our end of the horseshoe comes the Harvard band, with its tail of undergrads, to face the enemy across the greensward. Terrific cheers from ourselves.

The fateful hour is imminent. It is time to unleash the dogs of war. Three flannelled figures leap out in front of the Princeton host. They shout through megaphones to the enemy. They rush up and down the line, they wave their arms furiously in time, they leap into the air. And with that leap there bursts from twenty thousand throats a barbaric chorus of cheers roared in unison and in perfect time, shot through with strange, demoniacal yells, and culminating in a gigantic bass growl, like that of a tiger, twenty thousand tigers leaping on their prey—the growl rising to a terrific snarl that rends the heavens.

The glove is thrown down. We take it up. We send back yell for yell, roar for roar. Three cheer-leaders leap out on the greensward in front of us, and to their screams of command and to the wild gyrations of their limbs we stand up and shout the battle-cry of Harvard. What it is like I cannot hear, for I am lost in its roar. Then the band opposite leads off with the battlesong of Princeton, and, thrown out by twenty thousand lusty pairs of lungs, it hits us like a Niagara of sound. But, unafraid, we rise like one man and, led by our band and kept in time by our cheer-leaders, gesticulating before us on the greensward like mad dervishes, we shout back the song of "Har-vard! Har-vard!"

And now, from underneath the Stadium, on either side there bound into the field two fearsome groups of gladiators, this clothed in crimson, that in the yellow and black stripes of the tiger, both padded and helmeted so that they resemble some strange primeval animal of gigantic muscular development and horrific visage. At their entrance the megaphones opposite are heard again, and the enemy host rises and repeats its wonderful cheer and tiger growl. We rise and heave the challenge back. And now the teams are in position, the front lines, with the ball between, crouching on the ground for the spring. In the silence that has suddenly fallen on the scene, one hears short, sharp cries of numbers: "Five!" "Eleven!" "Six!" "Ten!" like the rattle of musketry. Then—crash! The front lines have leapt on each other. There is a frenzied swirl of arms and legs and bodies. The swirl clears and men are seen lying about all over the line as though a shell had burst in their midst, while away to the right a man with the ball is brought down with a crash to the ground by another, who leaps at him like a projectile that completes its trajectory at his ankles.

I will not pretend to describe what happened during the next ninety thrilling minutes—which, with intervals and stoppages for the attentions of the doctors, panned out to some two hours—how the battle surged to and fro; how the sides strained and strained until the tension of their muscles made your own muscles ache in sympathy; how Harvard scored a try and our cheer-leaders leapt out and led us in a psalm of victory; how Princeton drew level—a cyclone from the other side!—and forged ahead—another cyclone—how man after man went down like an ox, was examined by the doctors and led away or carried away; how another brave in crimson or yellow leapt into the breach; how at last hardly a man of the original teams was left on the field; how at every convenient interval the Princeton host rose and roared at us and how we jumped up and roared at them; how Harvard scored again just on time; how the match ended in a draw and so deprived us of the great carnival of victory that is the crowning frenzy of these classic encounters—all this is recorded in columns and pages of the American newspapers and lives in my mind as a jolly whirlwind, a tempestuous "rag" in which young and old, gravity and gaiety, frantic fun and frantic fury, were amazingly confounded.

"And what did you think of it?" asked my host as we rattled back to New York in the darkness that night. "I think it has helped me to understand America," I replied. And I meant it, even though I could not have explained to him, or even to myself, all that I meant.

— *reprinted from* <u>Windfalls</u> *by A. G. Gardiner (New York, J. M. Dent & Sons Limited, 1920); by permission of the publisher*

Shortly after leaving Princeton in 1923, Philip Wylie worked for two years on
editorial staff of the New Yorker *and was advertising manager of Cosmopolitan Bo*
Corporation in 1927 and 1928. Since 1930 he has been a very successful writer.
addition to numerous essays and short stories which appeared in Redbook, *the* Satur*
Evening Post, *and* Reader's Digest, *he has published many books, including* W*
Worlds Collide, Finnley Wren, The Big Ones Get Away, Generation of Vipe*
An Essay on Morals, Disappearance, Tomorrow, *and* The Answer.

Wylie is a member of the International Game and Fish Association, the Audu
Society, the Outdoor Writers Club, and Anglers, Incorporated. His many awa
include an honorary degree from the University of Miami, the Freedom Foundat
Gold Medal (1953), and the Henry H. Hyman Memorial Trophy (1959). All t
gives some indication of the varied aspects of contemporary life in which Wyli
interested. He writes of individual freedom and responsibility, the outdoors, deep-
fishing, American manners and morals, education, and the threat posed by new weap
of war, including the hydrogen bomb.

In the essay that follows, Wylie is arguing that the individual should have so
right to learn by experience, even though he may make mistakes while he is learni

(1902-   )

PHILIP WYLIE

One of Wylie's favorite crusades has alw
been directed against the domination
parents, particularly mothers; he is vigorou
opposed to what he calls "momism."

Safe and Insane

1

The past fifty years of what we call civilization have utterly ruined childhoo
The automobile, by restricting children to the yard or the block, by co
ditioning their very impulse to chase a ball, and by hooting at them lik
beast whenever they appear on the margins of its sacred raceways, has tak
away their last rights. The city itself is, of course, no place for childr
Today the millionaire's son is as much immured as the child in Victori
slums; perhaps the chauffeur drives him to and from school, but he is wall
in by the hooting iron and is altogether cut off from Nature.

The needs of children are perfectly described by those recent psychologi
discoveries which show that the development of each person follows t
evolution of the entire species. The infant is the instinctual animal; t
tot, a savage with the savage's fears, curiosities, unwitting cruelties, a
naïveté; the grade pupil is the advancing barbarian, full of lawless enterpris
excitements, rituals, outdoor achievement, and tribal activity; the adolesc
is the medieval mystic; after him comes the adult—*if* all the other sta
have been thoroughly experienced and assimilated. But in the modern ci

suburb, town, and even to a great extent in the village, the child has been deprived of any normal opportunity to engage in these cultural phases.

There is no adequate way for children to wage war against this fierce and universal imprisonment. Their parents try increasingly to barricade them from perils, to fence up their schoolyards, and to hire more supervisors for them, more lifeguards, more cops at corners, more counselors at camp. Their own so-called adult properties and interests constantly militate against childhood necessities. Their very working hours and pastimes make children a handicap rather than an interest. Indeed, the American child is impounded as soon as it can crawl in what is wretchedly called a play pen—a convenience to every mother, which keeps the tot from chewing through electric wires and the like, but which frustrates its every vital instinct.

The expression of natural instincts in towns and cities, limited to the unnatural material at hand, is necessarily of an "illegal" nature. In open country—woods, fields, farms, lakesides—the world is every child's oyster. In towns and cities, everything is "owned" save that which lies in the gutter. This presents the child with total dilemma, total frustration. His environment ought to belong to him and he ought to be a free agent in it. But if he even takes the bark off a tree to make a miniature boat to float in a pool, the urban child destroys somebody's birch, his dad has to pay, and the old lady who owns the goldfish pond has him chased by policemen.

The rebellion of city children naturally takes the form of property destruction, for property has become their enemy instead of their friend. They steal from stores; they steal cars; they smash windows; they set fires; they interfere with traffic; they damage trees and public benches; they paint brick walls and iron deer. Most of these are enterprises in which I, myself, have engaged. Generally, I was not caught; when I was caught, my family could pay. But the children of families who cannot pay, when caught in such activities and others analogous, are known as juvenile delinquents, taken before judges, sent to reform schools, and cemented into criminal habits.

Such rebellion, however, is merely a negative act which expresses resentment over the fact that the child has been deprived of all suitable opportunity to practise his impulses. The child of modern civilization takes his real revenge—or makes his compensation—when he has shaken off the trap of youth and has become, legally at any rate, an adult. The great majority of Americans alive today are preoccupied with such acts of revenge and compensation. They are performed in three principal categories, besides outright criminality.

The overweening passion of grown Americans for games, play, pleasures, and vicarious sports via stadiums, ball parks, radio, movies, and newspapers is the first great evidence of misspent—or, rather, unspent—childhoods. The second is the aggressive, hostile, irresponsible exploitation seen so commonly in businessmen—the littlest along with the greatest. Disguised as "go-getters," "individualists," "builders," and "progressives," they usurp as much power as they can, with total disregard for human welfare—as a revenge for and a protection against the damage society did them in childhood. They feel that by becoming owners they can make up for having lived for many years amidst universal deprivation. The third category results from a complete ruin of the adult by the distortions of childhood environment, and in it are some twenty per cent of the population: the hopeless neurotics and the insane. These people are popularly supposed to be unable to face the grown-up world; actually, they are unable to face the terrible destitutions of their childhood.

Children have been sacrificed to "civilization" as much as if they had been poured by millions into the belly of a red-hot idol. The cost, as any good psychologist would expect, is to be found in the national pall of adult infantilism and regression. Most adults remain children all their lives, often even those who are known as statesmen, senators, generals, admirals, and industrial tycoons.

The life of a child ought to be a process of adventure, experience, and exploit, graduated upward to suit his rising consciousness—which, as I have said, follows the unfolding pattern of all instinct. In this process, if he is to become truly adult and thus mentally and emotionally secure, he must make contact with the evolutionary experiences of his forebears, for only thus can his emotions mature and only thus can he get a biological sense of those fundamentals of human life and society which sustain civilization even at its most citified summits. But instead of aiding and abetting this procedure, we have done everything we can think of to shield and protect our children from the facts of life.

2

All my adult life I have been appalled at the absence of basic experience in my associates. They think they know what they are doing, but they live in a world of dreams; and the very fact of their ignorance inevitably fills them with enormous hostilities and with immense insecurities.

I have met countless people who are active in various health, hospital, welfare, and hygiene societies, but who have never seen a chicken killed or a kitten born. They cross the Atlantic, but they cannot swim. They have slept in hotels in Cairo and Bombay but never in the woods. They drive to the top of Pike's Peak, but they have never shinnied a tree or climbed a cliff. They install automatic heating plants in their homes and air conditioning in their offices, but they could not be trusted to burn trash in a back yard. They can make ice in their kitchens, but they have never skated or skied or showshoed. They eat all their lives, and wear carnations and orchids, but they have never planted a seed or raised a crop.

Now, these people, for all their wonderful accomplishments, such as the atom bomb, are not really conscious, because they have had no true primary experiences in life. They do not know what it is like to feel alive or to be alive. All of them are terribly frightened of their civilization. Their fears run from an entirely rational anxiety about crossing their own streets to the equally rational panic over the possibility that they may get into another war. Such fears, of course, make them aggressive—which greatly increases the chances of wars. They vacillate between worry and escapist work and play. They are, that is, supremely childish.

Communism and fascism, from this point of view, merely represent attempts to manage the increasingly infantile behavior of all people in our increasingly industrial societies. They are systems of treating adults as permanent children—of making the state into a universal father and mother; systems of ruling populations by absolute authority (by cajolery on the one hand and physical punishment on the other) not only over the activities of every individual but over his mind and his emotions as well. And the more childish we Americans become in compensation for our destruction of American childhood, the more vulnerable we become to some form of state absolutism.

Most of this change took place in my own lifetime, and today most parents are themselves the products of the sort of background I have described. The fears they feel concerning the world they do know are projected ignorantly, hence doubly, upon that normal, real, and natural childhood environment of which they lack the knowledge. Thus they keep eliminating, forbidding, and discouraging the very sorts of activity which are essential for youngsters. This is done in the name of safety and sanity. Its purpose is to protect the young from danger and from shock—such shock that is, as would upset these very unstable and subnormal adults. Actually, of course, the adult world is more terribly dangerous than it ever was in history. Actually, ignorance itself is dangerous, and the only hope of security lies always in understanding. And actually, of course, it is dangerous every minute to be alive anywhere at any time.

A normal childhood is normally dangerous. It is only through an experience of dangers, graduated to his age, that any child can grow up emotionally. Excessive protection is, for him, famine. A real adult will have real self-reliance and true independence, and will be deeply trustworthy, only if he has successfully passed through a great many experiences in which his own mistake could have caused his serious injury or even his death. A human being who has never had such experiences is likely, for instance, to be unqualified even to drive an automobile, since it represents the constant equation of "error equals injury and death." However, for the sake of adult convenience, of adult "freedom from worry"—and because of the projection of adult neurosis on childhood—safety and protection have been legislated into childhood to a degree that is murderous of adult personality. Not only are the unnatural restrictions of the city and town placed upon the youngster, but to them are added all the sickly prejudices, squeamishnesses, and ignorant dreads of the average urban parent.

Our "safe and sane" Fourth of July is an example. It is true that fireworks used to maim and kill children. Not many—as child-killing goes in this nation—but a few. There are, however, no statistics to show how many children who would have been maimed and killed because of their ignorance, poor instruction, untrained recklessness, and general incompetence in using fireworks were saved by the ban. Quite likely, the majority of all such still do get maimed and killed from other causes: falling off the backs of hopped trucks, setting fire to themselves, drowning, and other little dooms that are reserved for the ignorant, stupid, over-reckless, and incompetent among youngsters as amongst us all.

The institution of the "quiet Fourth" destroyed the greatest and most emotionally potent national fiesta America ever had. Its ceremony was handed down through generations. My father saluted sunrise on Independence Day with a brass cannon charged and fired by himself. He worked and saved to set rockets spattering the high dark of every July Fourth night. Bands, parades, and oratory were part of the celebration and they tied his emotions, by music, sights, and words, to the stirring deeds of his Revolutionary forebears. But the seal on that relationship was made by Father's own loud, glamorous, explosive *participation* in the proudest and most important memory we Americans possess.

I was taught, at a very early age, to shoot off fireworks. Little fireworks at first, big ones in later years, and rockets and Roman candles when I was ten. The Fourth of July was the day of my greatest boyhood independence. I was allowed public sanction to help wake up the whole town at the crack of dawn. I was permitted all day to make as much noise as I pleased. At night, it was my privilege to play gorgeously with fire. Instinct, tribal custom, fundamental human culture, here bound me gloriously to a supreme tradition of the fight of a bold people for liberty. In the whole adventure of being a boy there is no event so altogether satisfactory as a proper Fourth of July; the ritual is primitive and valuable beyond price.

When I was twelve, we moved to another State and the Fourth of July became a Boy Scout parade in hot uniforms, a lot of speeches, formal wreath-laying—in, of all places for such a day, a cemetery!—a long walk home, a late dinner, and fireworks distantly viewed that evening in a park.

In my thirteenth year, I accidentally discovered at a public library in this benighted State a book which told how to make black powder. I was not permitted by the librarian to take out this book on my card; so, naturally, I took it out under my coat—for good. In three different drugstores I purchased sulphur "for the roses," potassium nitrate "for the plants," and powdered charcoal "for dad's indigestion." These, when mixed according to directions, gave off a fine flash. I then made a cannon by boring an oak block in the manual training shop, loaded it with my powder, packed it with toilet paper and blue stone from the driveway, and touched it off by lighting a newspaper.

The first explosion was slow but fiery. After further reading, however, I caught on to such ingredients as potassium chlorate—then in use as a gargle—tannic acid, and other substances. And my extreme delight can be imagined when, one day, the charge in my gun gave a mighty bang and the chipped stones smashed several cellar windows in the house next door. Father paid for the windows.

Chapters from the story of my childhood usually cause my present friends and acquaintances to gasp with anxiety or even to snort with unbelief. Of what they consider perils and hardships, onerous duties and inordinate responsibilities, I had a far greater share than most of my friends. My busy parents let me go my way—even urged me to take chances when I was reluctant; but they saw to it, first, that I had the knowledge and the disciplines necessary for the undertakings. That is the point. I lived a great deal in the out-of-doors when I was young—and that is where all mankind lived for a million years and until the few last unsatisfactory thousands of years.

I should like to point out to every protective mother and father that, while I got hurt many times—cut, skinned, bruised, sprained, and so on—through independent acts, the most careful supervision failed to spare me from harm. My worst burn was sustained when, a baby in my mother's arms, I reached out as she stirred jam stewing on a wood stove and pressed my hand into its white-hot surface. My worst hurt occurred when I was about four and my grandmother was bathing me, standing, in a washbowl; somehow she let me fall. And the closest I ever came to death—during my protracted period—resulted from a bellyache for which my parents innocently called an old-fashioned osteopath. On three successive days he treated, by kneading, what had been from the start a ruptured appendix. I sustained my only severe fracture during a school gym period.

3

A great deal of attention has been paid by psychologists to the early sex training of children. Freud's discoveries have shown how crazily we behave in the dominant aspect of life. But it is only part of the background of childhood, one facet in the direct contact with Nature which the child requires. Sex difficulties, of a certainty, are the commonest expression of our modern human incompetence. But beneath them lies the fact that the form and purpose of the last few millenniums of man's development have been increasingly hostile to every opportunity for natural childhood.

Modern educators have followed the lead of modern psychologists and have attempted to set up systems which would give room for the development of the child's ego in relation to its playmates and to mother-child-father situations. In some schools, all formal discipline has been abandoned to "liberate" young personalities. This is futile. The one discipline which the child is emotionally equipped to learn, and indeed must know to live successfully as an adult, is the natural discipline of cause and effect—the perfect honesty of Nature and the absolute inviolability of its laws. For in natural law is the basis of all human morality; but because it can be assimilated only through experience, we regularly observe—with absurd regret—that there seems to be no other way by which each generation can learn anything. The regret is absurd simply because it arises from our fallacious notion that somehow civilization could or should reach the child vicariously, without risk to it or worry or bother to its parents.

The fact is that nearly all the properties, buildings, streets, machines, gadgets, higher courses of learning, governments, armies, navies, weapons, monetary systems, and other "advanced" aspects of civilization are superficial to *life*. Indeed, people who lack them all seem to be both wiser and more contented than the average American. To a child, these things are *totally* superficial—wretched excrescences that filch his necessary environs and replace them with deadly walls. To think, as parents do, that children can be morally educated and emotionally prepared for maturity in such a setting, and by means which substitute, at best, supervised samplings of natural life for the child-long experience of it, is like thinking that a man could be prepared to live on Mars by occasional squints at the stars.

Essays such as this are, by "civilized" custom, supposed to conclude with neat plans to solve any difficulties or problems which they present. Obviously, the cardinal idea here implied is that the entire way of life of Western man is wrong and has been wrong since before Greece and Rome. The reader, granting my premises, will hardly feel equipped to set out to arrest and redirect a process in being for thousands of years. Yet the reader, if a parent, can do precisely that within the limits of one family and perhaps with good effect on several families.

He can do it by understanding the true needs of childhood, by realizing that the needs are "rights," and by serving those rights above and beyond all other rights. Parents have no right, for example, to live in cities if they can possibly live outside them. Children have the right to observe and experience every fact of Nature—animal, mineral, and vegetable. They have a right to learn to be, step by step, independently able to live in natural environments. They have a right to take on such responsibilities as their age makes possible. They have a right to learn such truths and consequences as their emotional development permits, in environs that are not property— environs where they can dig, pluck, hoard, build, saw, cut, walk, swim, chop, paint, paddle, and pole without let or hindrance; environs where their normal impulse is neither inhibited by blue-jacketed guardians of every object nor confined by the artificial hazard of rushing, iron monstrosities. Children have the right to take, every day, such natural risks as their teaching in Nature gives them the competence to face.

Only that adult who is able to live successfully in a primitive world can bring enough knowledge and experience to civilized living to make it worthwhile. Without a realistic childhood background, he (or she) is a mere gadget himself. And a human being is not designed to be a by-product of a pile of buildings and a slew of machines or a parasite upon them.

I know that some readers, anxious mothers, will think this is a ghastly theory, and that I have never had charge of a child. The fact is, my brother and sister and I did most of the "bringing up" of our much younger half-brother and half-sister. The fact is that, as I write, my own daughter, who is fourteen, has just recovered from a badly broken arm which she sustained while riding a rough horse—I spent part of last summer encouraging her to ride by riding with her. I swam with her in "shark-infested waters," too, last summer. And when I found that she had gone swimming alone over the Bahama coral reefs, it gave me quite a turn. "I came in," she said, "when I looked down and saw an enormous purple sting ray right beneath me."

The reader will see that I have taught her to be prudent. And a few readers, perhaps, may see that my daughter has a good opportunity of growing into a person with some experience of Nature—and a fair quantity of self-reliance. Such, anyhow, is my hope for her.

— *first appeared in the Atlantic Monthly (January, 1948); reprinted by permission of Harold Ober Associates Incorporated; copyright 1947 by The Atlantic Monthly Company*

Bruce Hutchison was born in Prescott, Ontario, and educated in British Columbia. He worked as a journalist with the Victoria Times and the Winnipeg Free Press and has been editorial director for the Vancouver Sun since 1963.

The Incredible Canadian, a biography of William Lyon Mackenzie King, was published in 1932 and won a Governor General's award. Hutchison's interest in Canada, in government, and in Canadian-American relations has resulted in other well-known books, such as The Unknown Country: Canada and Her People (1943) and Canada— Tomorrow's Giant (1957), both of which also won Governor General's awards. In addition, Hutchison has received a National News award, the President's Medal from the University of Western Ontario, the Lorne Pierce Medal for Literature,

(*1901-*)

BRUCE HUTCHISON

and an honorary doctorate of Laws from the University of British Columbia. His novel, The Hollow Men, was a Book-of-the-Month Club selection in 1944.

The Canadian Personality

Somewhere across this broad land of Canada tonight there is a lost and desperate man trying to find the smallest needle in the largest haystack in the world. He is one of the best American journalists in the business, he has covered important stories in countless countries, but his assignment in Canada has stumped him. His assignment is to discover, analyze, and spread on paper for the American public, the inner meaning of Canadian life.

Well, I did the best I could for the poor fellow. I talked to him all last night but when I had finished he was still pacing my room, aflame with the mystery of his mission and certain other stimulating refreshments I had provided—he was pacing the room at dawn and complaining that I had really told him nothing of Canada. "What I have to find," he cried out in his agony, "is the Canadian character, the Canadian personality, the Canadian dream."

When I last saw him, staggering into the sunrise, he hadn't found what he was looking for. And it suddenly occurred to me that I hadn't found it either, after half a century, that I probably wouldn't find it, that it may be forever undiscoverable. I am not surprised, therefore, when my American friend concludes that there actually is no Canadian character, personality, or dream.

Nevertheless, he was wrong. But he set me thinking. And the more I thought about this thing the more confused I became. Yet he was wrong.

Now, it's true that you can't define the Canadian character, or at least I can't, nor can any of our statesmen, writers, or artists, so far as I have seen. But nothing of importance in life is definable. Once anything yields to definition you can be sure it isn't very important.

So we needn't go on making excuses, as we always do before strangers, because we cannot spell out the life of Canada like a chemical formula. And we shouldn't apologize either because the character of Canada is so divided and complex, holding within itself at least six sub-characters—the proud, grim, and inflexible character of the Maritimes; the gay but hard and practical character of Quebec; the bustling, able, and rather provincial character of Ontario; the character of Toronto, a growth so rare and baffling that I shall not venture, as an outsider, to give it even an adjective; the spacious, generous, and almost naïve character of the prairies; the boyish, ravenous, and self-centred character of British Columbia.

Our national personality is split many ways. So is the personality of every great nation and every great man in history. Britain is commonly supposed to have the most settled and clear-cut character of any country, but set the Scotsman or the Welshman against the Englishman, set the cockney against the north-countryman, and you will observe the startling diversity and contrast of British life.

We Canadians worry too much about our diversity. For it is an illusion, very common with us, to imagine that a nation grows strong by uniformity. Why, in the basic and most essential unit of mankind, in the family itself, diversity is the surest sign of strength and talent, the best guarantee of unity. No man in his senses would try to make his children all alike, and would mercifully extinguish them at birth if he thought they would resemble him when they grew up. What folly it is, what a will-o'-the-wisp, what a national obsession, to imagine that we shall only achieve a true national character when we have at last turned out a generation as uniform as a package of chewing gum and about as durable.

Nevertheless, as my bewildered American friend told me, it won't do to say that Canadians have strong and varied local characteristics in different parts of the country. That won't prove the existence of a national character. You must be able to prove that throughout the country there are certain dominant, widely shared and fully accepted characteristics, instincts, and deep feelings—certain common denominators by which the intangible thing as a whole can be measured. That is where the argument about our national character always collapses, as I have seen it collapse, over and over again, usually late at night amid a despairing clink of glasses, from Victoria to Halifax.

It's no wonder that it's a difficult thing to clutch in your hand, the character of Canada; wonderful, rather, that there is anything to clutch. Wonderful for this reason: Whereas other nations of the past grew up in a world of watertight compartments, and hardened into individual shape before other nations could touch and dilute them, we began to build a nation here only a few years ago, in a new world, in a violent world revolution, in an age where all nations were being driven together, cheek by jowl, through the new means of transport, information, and propaganda. Our case was peculiarly difficult, much more difficult, for example, than Australia's, because we lived beside a great established nation, the most powerful magnet the world has ever known, and its ideas have washed in on us in a ceaseless tide. We were indeed, and are still today, like a youth starting out on his path, glancing over his shoulder at the ancient glories of his home in Britain or France and, when he looks ahead, dazzled by the glitter of the United States.

Despite everything, however, I think we can begin now to detect some of the special characteristics common to all Canadians, and add them up to something.

First, and most obvious, is our national humility. We are a people bounded on one side by the northern lights and on the other by an inferiority complex just as vivid, a people distracted by the mossy grandeur of the old world from which we came and by the power, wealth, and fury of our American neighbors. We are the last people to realize, and the first to deny, the material achievements of the Canadian nation, which all the rest of the world has already grasped and envied. Self-deprecation is our great national habit.

This is curious, when you come to think of it, because so many of us are of British origin. A few days ago a scholar from India wrote in the London *Times* that the English consider their primary national vice to be hypocrisy, but he said, "I must insist on first things first. The root and beginning is self-admiration, and hypocrisy only its most distinguished product." Now that's an interesting epigram but its reception in England is *more* interesting. In Canada we would resent it, but the English loved it. They have had so much experience, they are so sure of themselves, that they can laugh at the impudence of outsiders. We don't laugh because we lack any self-admiration, and we're not very good at hypocrisy, either. We are hurt by the foreigner's criticism because we have a sneaking suspicion that it must be true, suspicion that would not occur to an Englishman. Never has there been a people in all history which has accomplished so much as the Canadian people and thought so little of it. An Indian scholar won't find self-admiration here. He'll find self-apology written in big black letters across our Canadian map— no, not in big letters. We write everything small if it's Canadian.

This, perhaps, lies close to the root of another national characteristic— we are a conservative and steady people, hardly daring to believe in our own capacity in the more complex affairs of statecraft, afraid to test that capacity too far with new systems and experiments. The Canadian audience at a political meeting (a significant little test, if the glummest), is the most stolid and dead-panned ever known—a collection of dull and sceptical haddock eyes to daunt the boldest politician; and our politicians truly reflect us in their stodgy competence, their unvarying pedestrianism, their high ability, their positive terror of color and flair.

And we are a lonely people, isolated from one another, in a land where the largest city is a frail wink of lights in the darkness of the night.

Lonely, and awed by the immensity of space around us, by the cold sweep of the prairies, by the stark presence of mountains leaning upon us, by the empty sea at our door, and by the fierce northern climate, which colors and toughens the weather of our spirit. And we are closer to the soil still, all of us, even in our cities, than the people of any other great industrial and urban nation.

We are more aware than others of the central physical fact of the earth, of growth, of harvest and decay. This land sense dominates all our national thinking, our politics, our economic system, and our personal habits. It makes our artists instinctively rush out to paint, not the abstractions of other artists, but the hard material of rock and pine tree.

This deep instinct for the land, our constant feeling of struggle against a harsh nature—this and our concentration on the mere task of survival, must be one of the things that makes us an unimaginative people, prosaic, pitifully inarticulate, and singularly lacking in humor. (We haven't even developed the great Canadian joke yet or learned to laugh at ourselves.) It may turn out that we are really filled with fire, poetry, and laughter, which we have repressed, thinking it inferior to other peoples', and perhaps these things will erupt some day, with shattering violence. So far there has been hardly a rumble, nor any tinkle of a national song nor the vague shape of a national myth.

On the evidence so far you might almost say that we have constructed a national character by refusing to construct one. The great void almost becomes a solid thing, the vacuum begins to take on substance, the national silence begins to speak in a clear Canadian voice. We have taken a *nothing*— our pathological horror of expression—and erected a *something* which distinguishes us from all other people. This is not enough to make a character, I admit, but you won't find it anywhere else. And perhaps the refusal to admit achievement is an achievement in itself.

But there is something about us more important and more distinctive than any of these obvious qualities.

We are among the few peoples still in the first throes of collective growth. While older peoples have settled down and accepted certain conventions, conditions, attitudes, and limitations as permanent, we accept nothing, least of all limitations. We live in a constant expectation of change, which we don't particularly relish and rather suspect, but cannot avoid. We have, every one of us, the feeling that we are involved in a process of perpetual expansion, development, and revision, whose end we cannot see.

We have the feeling, not of an old and settled resident in his father's house, but of a young man building a new house for himself, without any clear plan in his head and wondering how large his future family will be.

Ours is the doubt and risk, but the unequalled satisfaction of the man who builds and makes something with his own hands, perhaps the best satisfaction that life offers; and this sense of being only at the beginning of things, this expectation of a greater structure still to be built—this, I think, is the universal and most distinctive feature of the Canadian. We are, above all, a building people, a nation of beavers.

But, my American friend says, all this does not add up to a national character, and hence he concludes there is none. All right, then. We have failed to define that character, as I told you we would. But consider this: We have built here against every obstacle of geography, economics, racial division, and the magnet of our American neighbor—we have built here the greatest nation of its population in all recorded history. How did we do it? Why didn't we break up into inevitable splinters, why didn't we throw in the sponge and join the United States long ago?

No political decision, no economic planning, will explain that. Something much more than politics or economics was at work—the unshakeable will to make a nation, a home, a life of our own, for which no inconvenience was too great, from which no temptation could swerve us—a dim, impalpable, and dumb thing beyond our power to express or even name.

There is the hard, silent, and unyielding core of Canada, the final mystery which, like all the other things that matter in life, like life itself, is forever inexpressible and can only be intimated in myths and parables which, so far, we have been too busy and too reticent to invent. They will come in time, but the thing itself which they will vainly try to voice, is already here, and has been here since Champlain shivered on the rock of Quebec, in that first cruel Canadian winter, and has been carried by every Canadian boy, dumbly in his heart, to the battlefields at the ends of the earth—this dream of high mountains and deep forests and prairie skies, of summer crops and winter snow, and Canadian ways, and all the vast compact of familiar, precious things, making up together the substance of Canada which, through more than three hundred years we have refused to abandon, to sell, or even to mention.

If this is not yet a rounded and settled national character, it is, assuredly, the soil out of which a character is growing as surely as a boy grows into a man. It has grown these last few years faster than we have stopped to realize—of which the best proof, perhaps, is that, as never before, we now pause in our huge labors to ask ourselves what we are and what we hope to be. We cannot answer yet, but we know that we have within us, as our fathers had, one dominant feeling which is so general and unquestioned that we take it for granted. We quarrel about methods, political theories, economic systems, but such things do not make up a national character. Our character is not being built on them but on something much larger, a truly common denominator, the space, the beauty, and the free life of Canada itself.

Well, I wonder what haystack my American friend is searching in tonight for a needle which he could not recognize even if he found it.

— presented as a radio talk by the CBC, September 1, 1948; reprinted by permission of the author

Summer's Madmen

After a winter of reasonable unity Canada is split, by June, into factions forever irreconcilable. Two distinct kinds of men, almost two different species, go their separate ways.

The orthodox and civilized live on as usual in town. The heretics, most Canadian of Canadians, begin the tribe's oldest summer ritual. With the overpowering impulse of the wild goose, the death wish of the lemming, they swarm to the wilderness.

Now, throughout the land, a mass migration is heading toward the summer shack. The student of our folkways will find on every road out of town a steady stream of cars overloaded with food, bedding, lumber, tools, paint, cement, and no one knows what else—more than enough, you would think, to sustain an army's campaign. All the passengers are bound for some quiet waterfront by the outer gate of paradise, for a dilapidated house of no conceivable value and thus valuable beyond price.

Some people say that Canada has contributed no great thing to the world's culture. They have overlooked the Canadian summer shack. No doubt other peoples have country resorts, perhaps better and certainly more elaborate than ours, but it can be proved, I think, that our shack is indigenous, peculiar, Canadian, and mad.

Though aliens may understand it and foreign architects despise it, though it may violate every rule of construction and defy the laws of gravity, the shack remains the truest symbol of Canadian civilization because, of course, it is a revolt against civilization at large. Moreover, it is a miracle.

The shack is usually made of cardboard, fastened to a rock by a few rusty nails, built like an incompetent swallow's nest or a gopher's hole, and supported by some obscure principle unknown to science. Like all durable things, it rests on the foundation of a dream. It is held together by nothing more than invisible hoops of pure affection and human faith—sufficient to resist not only the fierce Canadian winter but also the deranged climate of mankind.

A summer shackman sets out on a trail that may appear new, but is as old as the white man's life in Canada, a branch of Champlain's trail leading straight from Quebec. Every year since 1608 the first odyssey has been repeated.

The latest version differs superficially from the original, is commonly carried by an automobile rather than a birchbark canoe, but inwardly it is unchanged and unchangeable. A shackman seeks summer, as his fathers have always sought it, in the only place where the summer of Canada can be found.

As he emerges from the woods, he sees in his shack one of the few certainties left on earth. Empires may reel, stock markets fall, and bombs explode, but the shack will be there. It has been waiting patiently for its owner. Its windows light up at his approach with a glitter of welcome. Its monstrous shape is charged with memories of laughter, tears, and vanished children.

When, at the sacramental moment, the shackman finds a rusty key (secreted, last autumn, where anyone could find it), turns a broken lock, and shoulders open a warped door, he enters a dank, musty cell, like a mountain cavern or the lair of woodland beasts. But when the fire is lighted, the bedding dried out, and the first meal of summer cooked, the cell instantly becomes a cloister in the New Jerusalem.

Then begins the heretic's summer of freedom, which the orthodox would call a sentence of hard labor, a cruel, unnatural punishment; freedom to mend the ever-leaking roof, to paint the decaying boat, to fix the unworkable pump, to cut firewood, and perform that infinite toil of preparation which the summer guest will take as his due while complaining bitterly about the service. The freedom, in short, of voluntary servitude, the summer slave system of a free country.

Opening camp is not really a labor. It is a transfiguration. The shackman is so transfigured that the orthodox will hardly recognize him in a fortnight. For only here in the open, away from human beings, can a man rediscover his humanity and be himself, do what he likes, build what he pleases, and return to the wisdom of a child building sand castles and perceiving the ultimate.

The nation is safe in the hands of the species that made it in the first place of native materials. No doubts about the future alarm the shackman. He mends his roof as if it would last forever. He adds a clumsy porch as if he were building for the ages. He paints his water-logged boat as if it would carry him across the river of immortality. If the final bomb should drop and civilization perish, somewhere, somehow, a shackman and his wife will survive—the first Canadians and the last.

— *reprinted from* <u>Canada — Tomorrow's Giant</u> *(Toronto, Longmans Canada Limited, 1957); by permission of the author and the publisher*

Born in Washington, D.C., Frank Moore Colby graduated from Columbia University with an M.A. degree in political science, taught at his alma mater and at New York University, and spent many years editing the New International Encyclopedia and the International Year Book. His essays and book reviews were published in various

(1865-1925)

**FRANK MOORE
COLBY**

American magazines, including The New Republic, Vanity Fair, and Harper's. The brief essay that follows illustrates the epigrammatic style that characterizes many of Colby's essays and reviews.

The Pursuit of Humor

While we Americans can never have too much humor, we can hear too much about it. I once followed a long controversy on the subject in the newspapers, especially on the question whether women ever possess this quality in their own right. It was a very solemn affair and a little tedious. Running through it all was an undercurrent of irritability, for these people would insist on citing cases in point, and just as soon as any one is rash enough to illustrate what he means by humor all hope of a peaceful discussion is gone. It is a rule alike for man and author never to illustrate in this matter. Disappointment is sure to follow, and sometimes hate. Even George Meredith becomes an object of scorn when he gives us samples of Diana's jokes. A definite promise of humor is always irredeemable. Then there was an extreme jealousy among the disputants lest any one should seem to be claiming more than his share. First one would come out with a scientific definition of it and a general air of mastership. Then another would show him up as an impostor, and in so doing try and give the impression that he had a rather neat turn for it himself. Like all discussions of humor, it was strenuous and was accompanied by the sound of heavy blows.

Now it is the commonest thing in the world to hear people call the absence of a sense of humor the one fatal defect. No matter how owlish a man is, he will tell you that. It is a miserable falsehood, and it does incalculable harm. A life without humor is like a life without legs. You are haunted by a sense of incompleteness, and you cannot go where your friends go. You are also somewhat of a burden. But the only really fatal thing is the shamming of humor when you have it not. We have praised it so much that we have started an insincere cult, and there are many who think they must glorify it when they hate it from the bottom of their hearts. False humorworship is the deadliest of social sins, and one of the commonest. People without a grain of humor in their composition will eulogize it by the hour.

Colby

Men will confess to treason, murder, arson, false teeth or a wig. How many of them will own up to a lack of humor? The courage that could draw this confession from a man would atone for everything. No good can come from the mad attempts to define humor, but there might be some advantage in determining how people should behave toward it. The first law is that humor is never overtaken when chased, or propitiated when praised. It is the one valuable thing which it is worth no man's while to work for. If this could only be learned, one of the gloomiest and most nefarious of industries would be banished from the world.

So, whether it is a man or a woman, or a weekly paper or a department of a magazine, the best advice in case of a deliberate attempt in this field is to give it up altogether. No one with any tenderness of heart wants to be the witness of that awful struggle. When the laborers in this vineyard take pains they always give them. That is the unhappy result of these discussions and of our indiscriminate praise. Heavy-footed persons start off in pursuit and the underbrush of light literature is always crashing with the noise of their unwieldy bodies. What is gained by these periodical *battues?* No one ever bags anything, and the frightened little animal is more seldom seen than ever. People should be more cautious in what they say about humor. If there were less said about it there might be more of the thing itself, for the anxious seeker ransacks these discussions for guiding principles and starts grimly off on the trail. He becomes a quasi-humorist with a system. Is there anything worse? In spite of the service which real humor renders, one may honestly doubt whether it offsets the injuries committed in its name. There are people whom nature meant to be solemn from their cradle to their grave. They are under bonds to remain so. In so far as they are true to themselves they are safe company for any one; but outside their proper field they are terrible. Solemnity is relatively a blessing, and the man who was born with it should never be encouraged to wrench himself away. A solemn mind out of joint—that is what happens when the humorous ambition o'erleaps itself. It is the commonest of accidents in this hunting field.

And another rule worth observing is that humor never works well when harnessed to a grudge. A writer tried to put it to this use only the other day. His resolute attempt to make fun of his political enemies took the form of mentioning them one by one and remarking in each case that they were "positively funny." People often refer to others as "positively funny" when what they really want to do is to garrote them; as if a thing conceived in darkness and shapen in malignity became humor by the invocation of the name. This is worse than the ordinary style of pursuit. It is the press-gang method.

— reprinted from *Imaginary Obligations* by *Frank Moore Colby (New York, Dodd, Mead & Company, 1904); by permission of the publisher*

John Boynton Priestley was born in Yorkshire, and was the son of a schoolmaster. He served in the British infantry during World War I, was wounded three times, and received a commission. After the war he took honors in English, modern history, and political science at Cambridge, and began his career as a writer. His critical and biographical essays during the twenties were well received, and his first novel, The Good Companions (1929), brought him wide recognition, both in England and on this continent. His literary reputation has been maintained with the publication of other novels and several plays, including Dangerous Corner (1932), Eden End (1934), and I Have Been Here Before (1937).

Priestley is also well known for his talks and wartime commentaries on the BBC, and for his stimulating lectures on a variety of subjects. The whimsical commentary on report cards that follows was taken from a collection of Priestley's essays that carries the very appropriate title, Delight.

(1894-   )

J. B. PRIESTLEY

No School Report

We fathers of families have one secret little source of delight that is closed to other men. As we read the school reports upon our children, we realise with a sense of relief that can rise to delight that—thank heaven—nobody is reporting in this fashion upon us. What a nightmare it would be if our personalities were put through this mincing machine! I can imagine my own report: "*Height and weight at beginning of term—5 feet, 9 inches: 13 stone, 10 lbs. At end of term—5 feet, 8 inches: 14 stone, 2 lbs.* Note: Through greed and lack of exercise, J.B. is putting on weight and is sagging. He must get out more and eat and drink less. *Conduct*—Not satisfactory. J.B. is increasingly irritable, inconsiderate, and unco-operative. He is inclined to blame others for faults in himself. He complains of lack of sleep but persists in remaining awake to finish rubbishy detective stories. He smokes far too much, and on several occasions has been discovered smoking in bed. There is no real harm in him but at the present time he tends to be self-indulgent, lazy, vain, and touchy. He should be encouraged to spend some weeks this summer with the Sea Scouts or at a Harvest Camp. *Eng. Lang. and Lit.:* Fair but inclined to be careless. *French:* A disappointing term. *History:* Has not made the progress here that we expected of him. Should read more. *Mathematics:* Very poor. *Art:* Has made some attempts both at oils and water-colour but shows little aptitude. Has been slack in his Appreciation and did not attend Miss Mulberry's excellent talks on the Italian Primitives. *Music:* Fair, but will not practise. *Natural History:* Still professes an interest but finds it impossible to remember names of birds, butterflies, flowers. Has not joined in the Rambles this term. *Chemistry:* Clearly has no interest in this subject. *Physics:* Poor, though occasionally shows interest. Fails to comprehend basic laws. *Physical Culture:* Sergeant Beefer reports that J.B. has been frequently absent and is obviously far from keen. A bad term. *General Report:* J.B. is not the bright and helpful member of our little community that he once promised to be. He lacks self-discipline and does not try to cultivate a cheery outlook. There are times when he still exerts himself—e.g. he made a useful contribution to the end of term production of *A Comedy of Errors*—but he tends to be lazy and egoistical. His housemaster has had a talk with him, but I suggest that stronger parental guidance would be helpful, and is indeed necessary." And then I would be asked to see my father, and would find him staring and frowning at this report, and then he would stare and frown at me and would begin asking me, in his deep and rather frightening voice, what on earth was the matter with me. But it can't happen, not this side of the grave. I am knee-deep in the soggy world of greying hair and rotting teeth, of monstrous taxes and overdrafts, of vanishing friends and fading sight; but at least, I can tell myself delightedly, nobody is writing a school report upon me.

— *reprinted from Delight by J. B. Priestley (London, 1949); copyright 1949 by J. B. Priestley; reprinted by permission of A. D. Peters & Co.*

Robert Benchley was born in Worcester, Massachusetts. After attending Harvard University, he was successively a writer of advertising copy for the Curtis Publishing Company, a drama editor for Life magazine, a writer for the New York World and the New Yorker, and an actor in a number of short Hollywood movies, for which he wrote most of the scripts. His collections of short humorous essays were published under such titles as The Treasurer's Report, From Bed to Worse, My Ten Years in a Quandary, Inside Benchley, and The Benchley Roundup (edited by his son).

Though Benchley wrote on a wide variety of topics, some of his most entertaining pieces are those in which he assumes the role of either a well-meaning character unable to cope with everyday situations or a dispenser of weird information on subjects about which he pretends to be badly misinformed. These range from "how to" build bridges, "how to" understand international finance, and "how to" sell goods, to "how to" create literary masterpieces. In 1936 Benchley received an Academy Award for his short movie on "How to Sleep." The essay that follows may (or may not) provide speakers at graduations with some useful guidance on "how to" tell young men about "the Facts of Life."

(1889-1945)

ROBERT BENCHLEY

A Talk to Young Men

To you young men who only recently were graduated from our various institutions of learning (laughter), I would bring a message, a message of warning and yet, at the same time, a message of good cheer. Having been out in the world a whole month, it is high time that you learned something about the Facts of Life, something about how wonderfully Nature takes care of the thousand and one things which go to make up what some people jokingly call our "sex" life. I hardly know how to begin. Perhaps "Dear Harry" would be as good a way as any.

You all have doubtless seen, during your walks in the country, how the butterflies and bees carry pollen from one flower to another? It is very dull and you should be very glad that you are not a bee or a butterfly, for where the fun comes in *that* I can't see. However, they think that they are having a good time, which is all that is necessary, I suppose. Some day a bee is going to get hold of a real book on the subject, and from then on there will be mighty little pollen-toting done or I don't know my bees.

— "A talk to young men" by Robert Benchley from The Benchley Roundup (New York, 1927) selected by Nathaniel Benchley; copyright 1927 by Harper & Brothers; reprinted by permission of Harper & Row, Publishers

Well, anyway, if you have noticed carefully how the bees carry pollen from one flower to another (and there is no reason why you should have noticed carefully as there is nothing to see), you will have wondered what connection there is between this process and that of animal reproduction. I may as well tell you right now that there is no connection at all, and so your whole morning of bee-stalking has been wasted.

We now come to the animal world. Or rather, first we come to One Hundred and Twenty-fifth Street, but you don't get off there. The animal world is next, and off you get. And what a sight meets your eyes! My, my! It just seems as if the whole world were topsy-turvy.

The next time you are at your grocer's buying gin, take a look at his eggs. They really are some hen's eggs, but they belong to the grocer now, as he has bought them and is entitled to sell them. So they really *are* his eggs, funny as it may sound to anyone who doesn't know. If you will look at these eggs, you will see that each one is *almost* round, but not *quite*. They are more of an "egg-shape." This may strike you as odd at first, until you learn that this is Nature's way of distinguishing eggs from large golf balls. You see, Mother Nature takes no chances. She used to, but she learned her lesson. And that is a lesson that all of you must learn as well. It is called Old Mother Nature's Lesson, and begins on page 145.

Now, these eggs have not always been like this. That stands to reason. They once had something to do with a hen or they wouldn't be called hen's eggs. If they are called duck's eggs, that means that they had something to do with a duck. Who can tell me what it means if they are called "ostrich's eggs"?——That's right.

But the egg is not the only thing that had something to do with a hen. Who knows what else there was?——That's right.

Now the rooster is an entirely different sort of bird from the hen. It is very proud and has a red crest on the top of his head. This red crest is put there by Nature so that the hen can see the rooster coming in a crowd and can hop into a taxi or make a previous engagement if she wants to. A favorite dodge of a lot of hens when they see the red crest of the rooster making in their direction across the barnyard is to work up a sick headache. One of the happiest and most contented roosters I ever saw was one who had had his red crest chewed off in a fight with a dog. He also wore sneakers.

But before we take up this phase of the question (for it is a question), let us go back to the fish kingdom. Fish are probably the worst example you can find; in the first place, because they work under water, and in the second, because they don't know anything. You won't find one fish in a million that has enough sense to come in when it rains. They are just stupid, that's all, and nowhere is their stupidity more evident than in their sex life.

Take, for example, the carp. The carp is one of the least promising of all the fish. He has practically no forehead and brings nothing at all to a conversation. Now the mother carp is swimming around some fine spring day when suddenly she decides that it would be nice to have some children. So she makes out a deposit slip and deposits a couple million eggs on a rock (all this goes on *under* water, mind you, of all places). This done, she adjusts her hat, powders her nose, and swims away, a woman with a past.

It is not until all this is over and done with that papa enters the picture, and then only in an official capacity. Papa's job is very casual. He swims over the couple of million eggs and takes a chance that by sheer force of personality he can induce half a dozen of them to hatch out. The remainder either go to waste or are blacked up to represent caviar.

So you will see that the sex life of a fish is nothing much to brag out. It never would present a problem in a fish community as it does in ours. No committees ever have to be formed to regulate it, and about the only way in which a fish can go wrong is through drink or stealing. This makes a fish's life highly unattractive, you will agree, for, after a time, one would get very tired of drinking and stealing.

We have now covered the various agencies of Nature for populating the earth with the lesser forms of life. We have purposely omitted any reference to the reproduction of those unicellular organisms which reproduce by dividing themselves up into two, four, eight, etc., parts without any outside assistance at all. This method is too silly even to discuss.

We now come to colors. You all know that if you mix yellow with blue you get green. You also get green if you mix cherries and milk. (Just kidding. Don't pay any attention.) The derivation of one color from the mixture of two other colors is not generally considered a sexual phenomenon, but that is because the psychoanalyists haven't got around to it yet. By next season it won't be safe to admit that you like to paint, or you will be giving yourself away as an inhibited old uncle-lover and debauchee. The only thing that the sex-psychologists can't read a sexual significance into is trap-shooting, and they are working on that now.

All of which brings us to the point of wondering if it *all* isn't a gigantic hoax. If the specialists fall down on trap-shooting, they are going to begin to doubt the whole structure which they have erected, and before long there is going to be a reaction which will take the form of an absolute negation of sex. An Austrian scientist has already come out with the announcement that there is no such thing as a hundred per cent male or a hundred per cent female. If this is true, it is really a big step forward. It is going to throw a lot of people out of work, but think of the money that will be saved!

And so, young men, my message to you is this: Think the thing over very carefully and examine the evidence with fair-minded detachment. And if you decide that, within the next ten years, sex is going out of style, make your plans accordingly. Why not be pioneers in the new movement?

Born in New York City, Corey Ford attended Columbia University, and then embarked upon a career as a free-lance writer. For almost forty years his humorous essays have been appearing in American magazines, and they have been collected in books which carry such intriguing titles as Cloak and Dagger, The Horse of Another Color, How to Guess Your Age, The Office Party, Every Dog Should Have a Man, Never Say Diet, How Do We Feel This Morning? and Has Anybody Seen Me Lately? His Short Cut to Tokyo was published in 1943 when he was a colonel in the American Army Air Force.

As the titles indicate, Ford writes on a variety of subjects, including dieting, visiting the doctor, raising dogs, trying to participate in a conversation, learning to ski, taking pictures, and baby-sitting. Though he has never worked in a business office, some of his most pungently humorous essays are those in which he satirizes the infantile behavior and petty jealousies that reveal themselves during the office parties and picnics of the "L. C. Twitchell Company"—which his reader can assume represents many American business organizations. In the following description of the rituals associated with the outdoor barbecue, Ford's knowledge of family behavior is rather remarkable—his own wife and family are non-existent; he is a bachelor who lives in Hanover, Massachusetts, with only a very large English setter for company.

(1902-   )

COREY FORD

How to Build an Outdoor Fireplace

There's nothing like an outdoor fireplace right in your own back yard. After all, why take a two-week camping trip in order to sit on the damp ground, swat mosquitoes, and get smoke in your eyes? With a little effort, you can be just as comfortable at home.

Take the folks across the street from us named Towse. It seems Mrs. Towse decided it was a shame to eat inside in this nice weather, so they moved all the chairs and tables out onto the lawn. Then Mr. Towse decided it was too much trouble to run back into the house every time he wanted a cold beer, so they moved the refrigerator onto the lawn. Then they moved the television set onto the lawn because the little Towse boy didn't want to miss the Westerns, and somebody told Mrs. Towse that it was healthier to sleep outdoors, so they moved all the beds onto the lawn, and finally Mrs.

Towse decided they ought to have a roof over their heads in case of rain, so they moved the house onto the lawn. They're using the old foundation for an outdoor fireplace.

What happened to the Towses, I'm afraid, is happening all over the country. Everybody's going out these days, and nobody's coming back. Outdoor fireplaces dot the suburban landscape like bomb craters. Today a kitchen is just a place to borrow a frying pan from. A home is something you eat in back of. People have gone barbecue-berserk.

Trouble is that every man in his secret heart yearns to cook over an open fire. Give him a chef's hat and a long-handled fork, and he will turn out a charcoal steak or a dish of spareribs that will make his guests turn green with envy, or at least green. This desire dates back to his early boyhood days, when he used to roast potatoes in the coals. On the whole, his cooking hasn't improved much.

In building an outdoor fireplace, the first step is to select the proper site. Personally I would recommend a location over on the far side of your property, under your neighbor's bedroom window, because there's no sense in having a lot of cinders and soot drifting over your own lawn. Try to pick out a spot at the top of a slight rise, so that prostrate guests will roll *away* from the fire rather than *into* the fire. Last but not least, be sure to choose a sheltered site out of the wind, preferably right up against the woodshed or garage. Not only will this avoid sudden down-drafts which might blow ashes in your face, but it should insure a brisk blaze when the side of the building catches.

Once the location has been decided upon, the next step is to lay out the fireplace. This can be turned into a rather colorful little ceremony, with the children waving small American flags and the wife reading excerpts from a pamphlet entitled *How to Build an Outdoor Fireplace; or, George, You're Doing It All Wrong*, while the head of the house places a wooden stake in the ground, places his thumb on the top of the stake, and drives it in with his hammer. Three more stakes are set in a rectangle, and a piece of white cotton string is run around them and tied securely, at which point the wife decides that maybe we ought to put the fireplace behind that clump of lilacs instead, George, we'd get the afternoon sun that way and, besides, there's more protection from the street. The stakes are pulled up and relocated behind the lilacs, whereupon the wife taps her teeth thoughtfully with a knuckle and suggests that it might be better after all if we moved it a little nearer the kitchen, so we wouldn't have to carry things so far. The ceremony is concluded along about midnight with the aid of a pocket flashlight, after the wife has gone to sleep.

And now to dig the hole for your barbecue pit. This is one of the most fascinating steps in the whole process, because you never know what you're going to find when you start digging. An hour's excavation in the average back yard will yield such assorted relics as (1) a wheel off a roller skate, (2) the handle of a china cup—never the rest of the cup; just the handle, (3) a couple of old spark plugs, (4) a furry object which resembles a moldy piece of bread and which, on closer inspection, turns out to be a moldy piece of bread, (5) the key to the preserve closet you've been looking for since last spring, and (6) several broken sections of tile, owing to the fact that you have inadvertently dug up part of your neighbor's plumbing system. I have no idea who goes around at night planting all these things in people's lawns. My own explanation is that I'm living on the site of a prehistoric Aztec midden. Last year I reported this fact to the Smithsonian, and got my whole yard dug up for nothing.

Be sure to save all the items you unearth, because they will come in handy when you build your fireplace. Probably you will need to add a few good-sized rocks, which can be obtained by touring the adjacent countryside and filling your luggage compartment with boundary markers, old cornerstones, and sections of farmers' stone walls. Park the car in front of your house, grasp a large boulder firmly in both hands, take a deep breath, and stagger bowlegged across the lawn, stooping and placing it carefully beside the hole. At this point you will discover that something peculiar has happened to the small of your back and you cannot straighten up again. Continue walking in a stooped position across the lawn and into the house, reach for the telephone, and call up a man named Tony. For a modest fee, Tony will be glad to come over and build your fireplace for you.

So much for the technical instructions. Now for some tasty barbecue recipes. If the amateur chef will follow these instructions carefully he will turn out a meal that will not soon be forgotten, if his wife has anything to say about it. (If there's one thing that drives a man crazy, it's the way that women never follow recipes. The average wife has a drawerful of menus she's clipped from magazines and newspapers, but when it comes to cooking she shuts her eyes and adds a pinch of this or a touch of that and just enough salt to taste. This must be why you never see women working behind prescription counters in drugstores.) All these recipes have been thoroughly tested by our own staff of barbecue experts. Unfortunately I can't give you the results, because the doctors say they won't be back at work for a couple of weeks yet:

Grilled Frankfurters Place a hot dog on the end of a forked stick, hold it over the coals, and let it drop into the fire. Fish it out with the poker, blow out the flames, and hold it over the coals again until the stick starts burning. Fish around in the embers until you recover a charred object that is either the frankfurter or your forefinger, sprinkle it with wood ashes, rub it in sand, grind it under your heel, blindfold your guests, and serve.

Ford

Barbecue Sauce 1 qt. hot mustard
1 lb. red peppers, ground
1 dash battery acid
1 bottle household ammonia
1 jar vitriol
1 box dynamite caps

Dump ingredients into heavy iron caldron and mix together thoroughly with spoon, adding bits of broken glass, assorted carpet tacks, and a few broken heads of sulphur matches. Continue stirring until the spoon dissolves. Connoisseurs insist there's nothing like a hot barbecue sauce to cauterize the roof of the mouth so you can't taste what you're eating. . . .

Bean-hole Beans Dig a hole in the ground about two feet deep by three feet square. Open a can of baked beans by inserting point of can opener in top and cutting around the rim. Dump contents onto a plate, toss the empty can into the hole, and eat beans with ketchup.

Robertson Davies was born in Thamesville, Ontario. He graduated from Queen's University and did post-graduate work in Shakespearean studies at Oxford. After spending two years as an actor in England, he returned to Canada in 1940 and became literary editor of Saturday Night, and then editor and publisher of the Peterborough Examiner. Since 1961 he has been a professor of English at the University of Toronto and a member of the Board of Governors of the Stratford (Ontario) Shakespearean Festival Foundation.

In addition to several novels, including Tempest-Tost, Leaven of Malice, and A Mixture of Frailties, Davies has written a number of plays and a collection of literary essays entitled A Voice from the Attic. In collaboration with Tyrone Guthrie, he wrote three books describing the first three seasons of the Stratford Festival Theatre.

In The Diary of Samuel Marchbanks, from which the following paragraphs were taken, Davies presents "a record of the daily life of a Canadian during one of the early years of the Atomic Age." The entries in the diary, some of which are reprinted here, are perceptive, witty comments on a variety of subjects, including politics, income tax, books, plays, elections, dogs that are too friendly, and a fiery monster over which Marchbanks has no control—the furnace in his basement.

(1913-   )

ROBERTSON DAVIES

From "The Diary of Samuel Marchbanks"

VII, SATURDAY: Was talking today to a man quite High in the Civil Service about censorship of books and put my question to him: What do the censors know about literature and, specifically, how can they decide whether a book is fit for me to read or not? I expected him to confess that the censors knew nothing, but instead he told me that the censors have a long and special training: first of all they attend a series of lectures on Sin, delivered by unfrocked clergy of all denominations, then they pursue a course of reading which comprises most of what is to be found on the Reserved Shelves of university libraries (the books you can't get unless you know the librarian or his secretary); then they travel widely, taking in the spicier entertainments of Naples, Port Said, and Bombay; then they are brought back to Canada, and if they still wear bedsocks, and blush deeply whenever they pass a cabbage patch or a stork in mixed company, and are able to tame unicorns, they are decorated with the Order of the Driven Snow and given jobs in the censorship department.

XIII, FRIDAY: Went today to view the X-rays which were taken of my inside some weeks ago. They were hung up on a rack and lighted from behind. I saw what was wrong at once; a long, thin, jagged monster was gnawing at my vitals; it was at least two feet in length, and on every joint there was a cruel hook. The doctor was very kind. He showed me my pylorus, and commented pleasantly on the nice appearance my spine made in the picture. But I could not take my eyes off the monster. Was it a tapeworm? Or was it something infinitely worse—something hitherto unknown to science? How long could I last with a thing like that in my vitals? As the doctor drew attention to the wonders of my inner world I grew more and more apprehensive, for I knew that he was saving the worst for the last. But the time came when he seemed to have finished. Summoning up all my courage, I asked the fatal question. "And that, doctor," I said; "what is that?" He lowered his voice, in case one of the nurses might overhear, "That is your zipper, Mr. Marchbanks," said he.

XVII, SATURDAY: Having averted my face from it for several weeks, I tackled the problem of Income Tax today. People of a mathematical turn of mind tell me that the forms are very simple if you attack them logically, but I am incapable of attacking an Income Tax form logically, or even coolly. Whatever my Better Self may say about citizenship and duty, my Worser Self remains convinced that it is a wicked shame that the government should take a big chunk of my earnings away from me, without so much as telling me what the money is to be used for. I know about the Baby Bonus, of course, but whose baby, specifically, am I bonussing with my money? Probably a damp, sour-smelling baby which I should hate if I met it face to face. Whose Old Age Pensions am I paying? Probably those of some lifelong prohibitionists, if the truth were known! People to whom I would not give a used paper handkerchief if I met them in the street are picking my pockets by means of this iniquitous Income Tax! The whole thing puts me into such a passion that I am incapable of adding and subtracting correctly. Clutching hands seem to snatch at me out of the paper until I scream and scream and scream.

XXIII, MONDAY AND ELECTION DAY: An election today, and everyone I met had a slightly woozy look, as though he had been sniffing ether on the sly. The streets were filled with cars, lugging voters to the polls; sometimes I wonder if that haulage business really pays; what guarantee does the free passenger give that he will vote for the man who provides him with a car? A really astute politician would send cars to pick up his known opponents, and would then carry them off, twenty-five miles or so into the country, and jettison them. Few of them would be able to walk home before the polls closed.——After the results were announced I was interested to see the wonderful unanimity of feeling which prevailed: the winning side was disposed to be generous, and told the losers that they wished they had done better; the losers, on the contrary, assured the winners that they had foreseen what would happen, and were in no way cast down by it; the socialists, who had been telling the world that they would win, proceeded forthwith to explain that they never dreamed of winning, and expressed delight that they had received any votes at all. Every one was so anxious to show complete satisfaction and good fellowship that a stranger, dropped by a parachute, would have assumed that they were all on the winning side.——The losers' hangover will begin tomorrow, when the ether wears off.

XXXV, THURSDAY: I see that Alfred Hitchcock intends to make a film version of *Hamlet*, only he will change it about considerably, and will leave out the poetry; Cary Grant is to star in this masterpiece. I can just see it; Hamlet will no longer be a Prince, but a truck-driver in a small American town; he will be ultra-democratic, and everybody will call him "Ham." His Mom will have bumped off his Pop in order to marry his uncle Claudius who thereby inherits the trucking business. Ham and his pal Horatio, and Ophelia (who is Ham's sugarpuss), will uncover this dirty work by showing Mom and Claudius some home movies of a similar case. Ophelia will have comic scenes with an undertaker, but will not really die, because she will have to marry Ham in the last reel, and help him with his trucks. Ham and Ophy may even have a screwball sequence in which they both pretend to be crazy, because everybody thinks craziness is so cute these days. It's a natural!——Of course, the Hays Office could never permit a film version of the Shakespearean *Hamlet*, because its theme is too closely bound up with incest to be tolerable to the pure minds of movie-goers. The movies insist that a good boy must love his dear old Mom, but wisely, and not too well.

XLIV, TUESDAY: Walked home this evening in the dusk, and passed a surprising number of couples of High School age conversing in low, tense voices as they leaned over bicycles or huddled under trees. Poets insist that Spring is the time of mating, but personal observation convinces me that the austere, bright nights of late Autumn are equally favourable to romance. The interesting thing about these lovers' conversations are the pauses. The lad asks some question which (to my ears, at least) has no amorous significance, and the girl then casts down her eyes, fingers her Latin Grammar in an agitated manner, and after a breathless interval (during which I try to keep on walking without getting out of earshot) replies, "Oh, I guess so," or "Oh, I just as leave," causing her swain to breathe hard and gulp.—— Why doesn't he throw himself on the ground, saying, "You are my Soul, my Better Self, be mine or I stab myself with this pair of protractors"; then she could reply, "Nay, press me not, I am Another's." In that way they could really have some romantic fun and store up things to tell their grandchildren. No style, no breadth, that's the trouble with the modern High School set.

XLVII, SATURDAY: Dashed out this morning to get some more Christmas cards; I am not what could be called a greeting-card type, but at Christmas I bow to the general custom. Saw a great many which inspired me with nausea, being depictions of jolly doggies hanging up their stockings, or pretty pussies doing the same thing; several cards were in what is called "the semi-sacred manner," showing the Holy Family with figures and postures strongly recalling the kewpies who used to appear in the advertisements of a famous tomato soup. St. Nicholas, too, appeared on many cards as a frowsy old drunk in a red ski suit, fingering his bulbous nose. In short, everything possible had been done to rob Christmas of its beauty, dignity, and significance. It was not in this spirit that Dickens wrote *A Christmas Carol*, and it is not in this spirit that I, personally, shall celebrate Christmas. I can stand almost anything except vulgar infantilism, and against that I shall war as long as there is breath in my body.

XLVIII, TUESDAY: Addressed Christmas cards tonight. There was a time when I used to hunt for the most suitable card for everyone on my list. I chose cards covered with lambs and reindeer for children, snow-scenes for friends who were wintering in Florida, High Church cards for friends of a ritualistic tendency, Low Church cards for evangelicals, Thick Church cards for those whose religion impressed me as a bit thick, cards with coaches and jolly drunken Englishmen on them for my jolly drunken American friends, and so forth. It was a lot of work, and I gave it up long ago. Now I buy my cards in large inexpensive bundles, and send them out in whatever order they happen to come.——Like everybody else I am sending cards this year to people who sent me cards last year, but whom I forgot last year, and who will not send me cards this year. This desperate game goes on for decades, and there seems to be no way of stopping it.——On several cards I put messages such as, "Why don't you write?" or "Am writing soon," which is a lie. I have no intention of writing them, but in an excess of Christmas spirit I pretend that serious illness, or the press of affairs, is the only thing which keeps me from sending them a long letter every week.

— *paragraphs from The Diary of Samuel Marchbanks by Robertson Davies (Toronto, 1947); reprinted by permission of Clarke Irwin and Company Limited*

Eric Nicol spent his infancy in Kingston, Ontario, and his boyhood and youth in Vancouver where he attended U.B.C., contributed to the campus paper, the Ubyssey, and completed an M.A. degree. Since graduation he has been a columnist on the staff of the Vancouver Daily Province, and his jesting accounts of people, places, institutions, and events are syndicated in many newspapers across Canada and the United States.

Though much of his writing is concerned with Canadian customs and attitudes, his topics are not bounded by the Canadian border. For example, The Roving I is an hilarious account of his travels through Europe—France in particular; Say, Uncle is his interpretation of American history and institutions; Russia Anyone puts a few dents in the "iron curtain." Eric Nicol has been awarded the Leacock Medal for his humor three times, and the end is not yet in sight; there are still ample topics, including money, television, and miniskirts, if he chooses to write about them, to provide him with the opportunity to make us laugh at our own behavior.

(1919-   )

ERIC NICOL

Love Affair

I have traded in the old ox-wagon on a later model. This car has all the new improvements, like cylinders and pistons and doors. When I go around a corner the back wheels follow the front wheels as nice as you please.

Naturally I am fiercely proud of the car. I resent every drop of rain that falls on its lovely burgundy body. The other night a young lady, in the excitement of the chase, put her shoes on the upholstery, obliging me to strike her senseless.

I live in terror of the first scratch. I buy ethyl gasoline containing alphabet. I pry tiny pebbles out of the tires, the first tires I ever owned that had tread.

I have also stopped eating in drive-in restaurants. I keep gagging on my bun every other time another car comes anywhere near my paint.

This feeling will wear off, of course. Already I've started letting passengers open their windows themselves. The first time somebody used the ashtray I bit my lip but I got over it. Anybody who drops ashes on the floor, however, is still handed a whisk, politely but firmly.

And I still thrill to the surge of power when I step on the accelerator. In the old car, stepping on the accelerator was mostly exercise for the right ankle. Now I barely have to touch the pedal and the old speedometer

— from Shall We Join the Ladies by Eric Nicol (1955); reprinted by permission of The Ryerson Press, Toronto

116

zooms up to thirty. The car doesn't seem to be going any faster, but that speedometer is obviously itching for the Salt Flats of Utah.

I guess the reason the car doesn't seem to be going as fast as the speedometer is the car rides so smoothly. Boy, you can just feel the air in those tires, *pounds* of it. (I get my air out in the suburbs, where it's nice and fresh.)

The old car had a terrible squeak in the door, but not this new car. This car does have a sort of high-pitched purr, at the back, that some people have mistaken for a squeak. It started just after the thirty-day guarantee was up. Myself, I find it a friendly sound, like a cricket on the hearth, or a sucker on the car lot.

The salesman who sold me the car placed his hand on a stack of the collected works of Machiavelli and swore that the car had been owned by an elderly couple who drove it in nothing but funerals. This lovely old couple, over the years, had tenderly put 96,000 miles on the car. The old lady was a dwarf who never got to sit on the seat, the salesman said. He was a friendly fellow, that salesman, putting his arm around my hips and patting my wallet.

After I had fallen in love with the car the salesman led me away to a little office where he took out a pad and a pencil. He had given me, by his own admission, a special price on my old car. The firm was flirting with bankruptcy. It wasn't until we went into the little office that the firm got a grip on itself and returned to its legally wedded larceny.

It was the "extras" that did it. For instance, looking at the car on the lot I hadn't realized that a steering wheel connected with the wheels was an extra.

"Do you want a battery with your engine?" the salesman asked.

I nodded, and he jotted down some figures, what looked like the monthly take of one of our senior banks.

What with one extra and another, the car cost more than I could really afford. But what's money when you're in love? She's mine, and we've yet to have our first quarrel. I'm driving with stars in my eyes.

E. B. White was born in Mount Vernon, New York, and served in the American army during World War 1. Later, he attended Cornell University, from which he graduated with an A.B. degree in 1921. After some experience as a newspaper reporter, he turned to free-lance writing. For thirty years his essays about the life and society of our time have appeared in the New Yorker magazine. He has also been a frequent contributor to Harper's.

White is one of America's most respected essayists, and has received honorary degrees from many colleges and universities, including Dartmouth, Maine, Yale, and Harvard. He is a Fellow of the American Academy of Arts and Sciences, and in 1963 was awarded the presidential Medal of Freedom. His collections of essays include Every Day is Saturday, Quo Vadimus, One Man's Meat, and The Second Tree from the Corner.

The two "letters" that follow tell us much about White's personality, his interests, and his attitudes toward certain aspects of our highly organized society. They also show why he is considered one of the most effective contemporary writers of crisp, lucid English prose. In an essay a few years ago criticizing a book designed to tell writers "how to write to be understood," White stated that "writing is an act of faith between writer and reader." He meant that the writer has to present his own ideas in the way he finds most effective, and he has to assume that the reader is intelligent enough and interested enough to read and understand the meaning of the work that the writer has created.

(1899-   )

ELWYN BROOKS WHITE

Two Letters, Both Open

New York, N.Y.
12 April 1951

The American Society for the Prevention of Cruelty to Animals
York Avenue and East 92nd Street
New York 28, N.Y.

Dear Sirs:

I have your letter, undated, saying that I am harboring an unlicensed dog in violation of the law. If by "harboring" you mean getting up two or three times every night to pull Minnie's blanket up over her, I am harboring

— two "letters" reprinted from The Second Tree From The Corner (New York, 1954) by E. B. White; copyright 1951 by E. B. White; originally appeared in the New Yorker, and reprinted by permission of Harper & Row, Publishers

a dog all right. The blanket keeps slipping off. I suppose you are wondering by now why I don't get her a sweater instead. That's a joke on you. She has a knitted sweater, but she doesn't like to wear it for sleeping; her legs are so short they work out of a sweater and her toenails get caught in the mesh, and this disturbs her rest. If Minnie doesn't get her rest, she feels it right away. I do myself, and of course with this night duty of mine, the way the blanket slips and all, I haven't had any real rest in years. Minnie is twelve.

In spite of what your inspector reported, she has a licence. She is licensed in the State of Maine as an unspayed bitch, or what is more commonly called an "unspaded" bitch. She wears her metal licence tag but I must say I don't particularly care for it, as it is in the shape of a hydrant, which seems to be a feeble gag, besides being pointless in the case of a female. It is hard to believe that any state in the Union would circulate a gag like that and make people pay money for it, but Maine is always thinking of something. Maine puts up roadside crosses along the highways to mark the spots where people have lost their lives in motor accidents, so the highways are beginning to take on the appearance of a cemetery, and motoring in Maine has become a solemn experience, when one thinks mostly about death. I was driving along a road near Kittery the other day thinking about death and all of a sudden I heard the spring peepers. That changed me right away and I suddenly thought about life. It was the nicest feeling.

You asked about Minnie's name, sex, breed, and phone number. She doesn't answer the phone. She is a dachshund and can't reach it, but she wouldn't answer it even if she could, as she has no interest in outside calls. I did have a dachshund once, a male, who was interested in the telephone, and who got a great many calls, but Fred was an exceptional dog (his name was Fred) and I can't think of anything offhand that he *wasn't* interested in. The telephone was only one of a thousand things. He loved life—that is, he loved life if by "life" you mean "trouble," and of course the phone is almost synonymous with trouble. Minnie loves life, too, but her idea of life is a warm bed, preferably with an electric pad, and a friend in bed with her, and plenty of shut-eye, night and day. She's almost twelve. I guess I've already mentioned that. I got her from Dr. Clarence Little in 1939. He was using dachshunds in his cancer-research experiments (that was before Winchell was running the thing) and he had a couple of extra puppies, so I wheedled Minnie out of him. She later had puppies by her own father, at Dr. Little's request. What do you think about *that* for a scandal? I know what Fred thought about it. He was some put out.

Sincerely yours,

E. B. White

New York, N.Y.
12 April 1951

Collector of Internal Revenue
Divisional Office
Bangor, Maine

Dear Sir:

I have your notice about a payment of two hundred and some-odd dollars that you say is owing on my 1948 income tax. You say a warrant has been issued for the seizure and sale of my place in Maine, but I don't know as you realize how awkward that would be right at this time, because in the same mail I also received a notice from the Society for the Prevention of Cruelty to Animals here in New York taking me to task for harboring an unlicensed dog in my apartment, and I have written them saying that Minnie is licensed in Maine, but if you seize and sell my place, it is going to make me look pretty silly with the Society, isn't it? Why would I license a dog in Maine, they will say, if I don't live there? I think it is a fair question. I have written the Society, but purposely did not mention the warrant of seizure and sale. I didn't want to mix them up, and it might have sounded like just some sort of cock and bull story. I have always paid my taxes promptly, and the Society would think I was kidding, or something.

Anyway, the way the situation shapes up is this: I am being accused in New York State of dodging my dog tax, and accused in Maine of being behind in my federal tax, and I believe I'm going to have to rearrange my life somehow or other so that everything can be brought together, all in one state, maybe Delaware or some state like that, as it is too confusing for everybody this way. Minnie, who is very sensitive to my moods, knows there is something wrong and that I feel terrible. And now *she* feels terrible. The other day it was the funniest thing, I was packing a suitcase for a trip home to Maine, and the suitcase was lying open on the floor and when I wasn't looking she went and got in and lay down. Don't you think that was cute?

If you seize the place, there are a couple of things I ought to explain. At the head of the kitchen stairs you will find an awfully queer boxlike thing. I don't want you to get a false idea about it, as it looks like a coffin, only it has a partition inside, and two small doors on one side. I don't suppose there is another box like it in the entire world. I built it myself. I made it many years ago as a dormitory for two snug-haired dachshunds, both of whom suffered from night chill. Night chill is the most prevalent dachshund disorder, if you have never had one. Both these dogs, as a matter of fact, had rheumatoid tendencies, as well as a great many other tendencies, specially Fred. He's dead, damn it. I would feel a lot better this morning if I could just see Fred's face, as he would know instantly that I was in trouble with the authorities and would be all over the place, hamming it up. He was something.

About the tax money, it was an oversight, or mixup. Your notice says that the "first notice" was sent last summer. I think that is correct, but when it arrived I didn't know what it meant as I am no mind reader. It was cryptic. So I sent it to a lawyer, fool-fashion, and asked him if *he* knew what it meant. I asked him if it was a tax bill and shouldn't I pay it, and he wrote back and said, No, no, no, no, it isn't a tax bill. He advised me to wait till I got a bill, and then pay it. Well, that was all right, but I was building a small henhouse at the time, and when I get building something with my own hands I lose all sense of time and place. I don't even show up for meals. Give me some tools and some second-handed lumber and I get completely absorbed in what I am doing. The first thing I knew, the summer was gone, and the fall was gone, and it was winter. The lawyer must have been building something, too, because I never heard another word from him.

To make a long story short, I am sorry about this non-payment, but you've got to see the whole picture to understand it, got to see my side of it. Of course I will forward the money if you haven't seized and sold the place in the meantime. If you have, there are a couple of other things on my mind. In the barn, at the far end of the tieups, there is a goose sitting on eggs. She is a young goose and I hope you can manage everything so as not to disturb her until she has brought off her goslings. I'll give you one, if you want. Or would they belong to the federal government anyway, even though the eggs were laid before the notice was mailed? The cold frames are ready, and pretty soon you ought to transplant the young broccoli and tomato plants and my wife's petunias from the flats in the kitchen into the frames, to harden them. Fred's grave is down in the alder thicket beyond the dump. You have to go down there every once in a while and straighten the headstone, which is nothing but a couple of old bricks that came out of a chimney. Fred was restless, and his headstone is the same way—doesn't stay quiet. You have to keep at it.

I am sore about your note, which didn't seem friendly. I am a friendly taxpayer and do not think the government should take a threatening tone, at least until we have exchanged a couple of letters kicking the thing around. Then it might be all right to talk about selling the place, if I proved stubborn. I showed the lawyer your notice about the warrant of seizure and sale, and do you know what he said? He said, "Oh, that doesn't mean anything, it's just a form." What a crazy way to look at a piece of plain English. I honestly worry about lawyers. They never write plain English themselves, and when you give them a bit of plain English to read, they say, "Don't worry, it doesn't mean anything." They're hopeless, don't you think they are? To me a word is a word, and I wouldn't dream of writing anything like "I am going to get out a warrant to seize and sell your place" unless I meant it, and I can't believe that my government would either.

The best way to get into the house is through the woodshed, as there is an old crocus sack nailed on the bottom step and you can wipe the mud off on it. Also, when you go in through the woodshed, you land in the back kitchen right next to the cooky jar with Mrs. Freethy's cookies. Help yourself, they're wonderful.

Sincerely yours,

E. B. White

Joyce Cary was born in Londonderry, Ireland, and spent a happy boyhood at Cary Castle, the centre of a large estate which had been held by his English ancestors for almost three centuries. After attending Clifton College in Bristol, Cary studied art in Edinburgh and Paris, and then completed a degree at Oxford University in 1912. After graduating, he participated in the Balkan War (1912-1913) and was decorated for bravery. During the next seven years he served with a Nigerian regiment in World War I and then became administrative officer for a large district peopled almost entirely by Nigerian natives.

In 1920 ill health resulting from overwork compelled Cary to leave Africa. He took up residence in a large Victorian house in Oxford and devoted the next ten years to study, research, and writing, as an apprenticeship to embarking upon a career as a novelist. With the exception of <u>The African Witch</u> (1936), which was a Book Society selection, his novels received little recognition until the period following World War II, when his trilogy, <u>Herself Surprised</u>, <u>To Be a Pilgrim</u>, and <u>The Horse's Mouth</u>, became popular in both Britain and America. Today Joyce Cary is recognized as one of the important writers of our time. When he died at Oxford in 1957, he had completed more than a dozen significant novels, as well as several books of non-fiction in which he discussed philosophy, the arts, and the barriers to human freedom.

(1888-1957)

JOYCE CARY

An excerpt from "Art and Reality"

. . . We can realise the power, day by day, of the press, the radio, the cinema. They are very obviously a great part of those creative forces which are changing the world all the time. Art, as creation in language, creates ideas, of which a very large proportion are, or become, ideas for action.

Of course, we have the best proof of the power of art in the fact that every dictator, every authority aspiring to complete control, from a church with its index to a local council that excludes the press, sets up a censorship. And the more determined the dictators, the more complete the censorship. Hitler and Stalin attempted to control all the arts: painting, sculpture, and architecture, as well as the art of the word.

*　　*　　*

The reason is that art expresses and communicates feelings and desires, and that men live by their feelings and desires. What they seek in life from the very beginning is to satisfy various appetites and emotional needs. For that they require an idea of the world in which they have to succeed, from which they have to obtain satisfaction. They want a guide to life as navigators want a map, so that they shan't run on destruction before they find port. Guides to life, however, even before they come to interpretation by the individual, differ so much that the young are apt to be bewildered. A good many give up all hope of any clear and reliable guide very early indeed, even in their teens. But the desire remains and it is very urgent. That is why any new creed presenting a complete guide is so sure of popularity among students, why Marxism, Fabianism, Nazism, spiritualism, any new "ism" which offers a complete picture, even a depressing picture, like Spenglerism or behaviourism, has such immense appeal to anyone under thirty. They set free; they give a coherent set of values, in which emotions formerly in conflict, and therefore frustrated, can suddenly find complete satisfaction. Everyone has noticed the self-confidence of the Marxist convert. The neurotic and frustrated muddle-head of a month ago, uncertain and bewildered in every contact, in every relation, has become completely sure of himself and full of eagerness to realise this world that he has now found, to realise himself, to enjoy himself in that world. That is why he is also indifferent to facts or argument. He does not accept any fact that would injure his new faith, in which alone he finds his way of life.

This desire for the guide, the clear picture which sets free, is so urgent that almost any dogmatic statement, so long as it is simple and clear, will be accepted. Tolstoy's anarchism carried such weight because it was the simplest of all. Tolstoy said in effect, do nothing, leave it all to God, who is found in our own human nature. This fiction carried a unique emotional appeal. It offered a golden age of peace and love and happiness, which was to be attained at once, much sooner than the Marxian. Tolstoy did not promise merely that the State would wither when evil had vanished from the world and all men were always good; he said that if the State were at once abolished, all men would be good, and universal happiness would begin.

In fact, men live so entirely by feeling that reason has extremely small power over even our most intelligent, our geniuses like Marx and Tolstoy. If you don't believe this, you only have to look at the papers, at day-to-day politics. We see there how little reason, how little even common prudence, can restrain whole peoples, or their leaders, from actions which amount to suicide when they are offered a chance of gratifying such entirely egotistic passions as greed, hatred, revenge, pride, wounded self-esteem or, most powerful, most persistent and most reckless of all, an inferiority complex. This is not to say that they are completely selfish. On the contrary, passions are often regardless of self; a man will cheerfully die for such an ideal and abstract notion as religious faith, a country which does not even exist except as a name, or merely for duty and honour, the good name of his regiment or family.

Thus the most important part of man's existence, that part where he most truly lives and is aware of living, lies entirely within the domain of personal feeling. Reason is used only to satisfy feeling, to build up a world in which feelings can be gratified, ambition realised; and, as we see in history, even then it has very little power in conflict with any strong emotion, any powerful symbol like a flag, the mere name of a country, even one invented last week, or words like "freedom."

The new inventions, radio and television, have enormously increased this turmoil, because they have increased the power of the world, of rhetoric, of the demagogue. And education, which is demanded by all peoples and provided by all governments, itself makes millions more restless, more dissatisfied, more ready to listen to the demagogues. Never before in history has the word, in speech and book, the picture on the cinema or on television, the dogma in some national or commercial slogan, had such power. And they have produced such a confusion of ideologies and militant nationalisms that a great many people despair of civilisation as it is. They expect the world to tumble once more into a thousand years of barbarism.

So we have new demands for censorship all over the world, and new censorships imposed by governments. Their excuse is always the same, that artists and writers distort the truth. But censorship in history always has the same result; sooner or later it produces corruption, frustration, and cynicism in whole peoples. It fosters the black-market of rumour and suspicion and undermines the State with secret hatred of all authority and, worse, contempt for its fears, a keen perception of its weakness.

A people treated like irresponsible morons will behave like irresponsible savages—the Teddy boy adolescent toting a spring-knife to swagger away his own miserable sense of ignorance and self-contempt is only the Teddy boy nation writ small.

To suppress the freedom of the arts is not only to cut off knowledge of the actual movements of human feeling but also, and more disastrously, contact with the realities of life. For those contacts can be renewed only by the continually new intuition of the artist.

— reprinted from <u>Art and Reality</u> *by Joyce Cary (London, Cambridge University Press, 1958); by permission of Curtis Brown Limited*

Born in Bloomfield, New Jersey, Randolph Bourne was a cripple, a misshapen dwarf who refused to let his physical deformity bar him from an active and productive life. With courage and energy and an alert mind, he completed both a B.A. and an M.A. at Columbia University and then studied in London and Paris on a post-graduate fellowship. He was one of the founders of The New Republic *and a frequent contributor to other leading periodicals of his time.*

Bourne's interest in youth and his hatred of war were expressed in Youth and Life *(1913) and* Towards an Enduring Peace *(1916). Two of his other books, entitled* Untimely Papers *and* The History of a Literary Radical, *were published after his death. In "What Is Opinion" Bourne expresses a philosophy that guided much of his writing: he says, "You do not revise dogmas. You smash them."*

(1886-1918)

RANDOLPH BOURNE

What is Opinion?

A journal of opinion has always to face the attack of the practical man that it is a mere vehicle for dilettantism, which wastes in expressing sentiments the energy which should go to the presentation of sober fact and sound data. There is far too much opinion at large in the world already, he thinks. What he wants is not more opinion, but a guide out of the fogbank into some clear light.

Such a practical man flatters too highly most of that comment which passes for opinion in the journals of the day. Most current reactions to the war have been, for example, not opinion at all, but mere batteries of guns in an emotional warfare. In all the discussion little emerges that is not articulate emotion or articulate group-interest. This variedly articulate anger, disgust, prejudice, moral reaction, has little more right to be termed opinion than the start one gives when one meets a bear. It is instinctive response clothed with words.

Our molders of opinion—our preachers and politicians and editors and publicists—are not speaking in order so much to convince us as to make us act or vote or feel with them. Their words are chains of phrases strung together almost undesignedly with a view to pulling us to the cause or party or idea they are supporting. It is a curious delusion that words express thought. The object of most words is to short-circuit thought. Phrases like democracy, liberty, militarism, the principles of justice and humanity, are not primarily meanings at all. They are epithets hurled at us to arouse some desired resentment, or they are spotlights guaranteed to create certain warm emotional glows of assent in the mind which receives them. It is the reaction they touch off that makes them significant, not their meaning. Words are such deadly things not because they mean something, but because they get wrapped up with our emotion and pull it out with them when they are seized. In support of the articulate emotion there may be any number of highly rational arguments. But it is not the arguments which have come first. It is the antagonism or the glow of approval, while the evidence has grown almost vegetatively around the emotion. The world is always willing to be fooled in this way. It is always willing to take the ideas at their face value, instead of going straight to the emotional core and discovering the animus that directed the collection of the ideas. The constant danger to the mind that would be intellectual, that would "have opinions," is that it is willing to identify itself or indolently let itself be identified with groups that are not expressing opinion at all, but only articulating their emotion.

Genuine opinion is neither cold, logical judgment nor irrational feeling. It is scientific hypothesis, to be tested and revised as experience widens. Opinion is a view of a situation based on grounds short of proof. In a valid opinion they must be *just* short of proof. Good opinion is not spasmodic. The mind must have made a very wide sweep, made the complete circuit of the compass. It must first have hunted down the predisposing prejudice and neutralized it, and then bent itself to discovering all the factors that converge upon the situation. A good opinion places the event or person or idea it is judging firmly in a scheme of things. You get its position in a spreading field as well as in a historical chain.

But good opinion is not flabby and uncertain. It is not a "much to be said on both sides." It is a provisional conviction to be held as a conviction until new light alters it. It is an interpretation with a definite slant and bias. But it presses hotly for proof. It strains constantly toward the accuracy of truth. Good opinion, although firm, is the direct opposite of dogma. Dogma is hard and unyielding, a sort of petrified emotion. It is constantly masquerading as proof, as genuine opinion never does. You do not revise dogmas. You smash them. But opinion is flexible and gracious. It does not object to examining itself, to publishing the source of its interpretations. It takes you freely behind the scenes. It is not afraid to show you the foundations of the categories and terms in which it is expressed. It will let the bony framework of its presuppositions stand out rather boldly at times. It invites criticism. It has the scientist's disinterestedness in its own conviction. What it wants is to understand, to get the thing it is judging rightly placed, to grasp its true meaning in the world.

Opinion, however, aims not at a mere static comprehension. It does not merely survey the field with serene Olympian gaze. It is a force, and the only force that can be relied upon in the long run to fortify the will and clear the vision. Conviction, gripped after the widest possible survey of the field, is what we must act upon if we are to effect those social changes which most of us desire. The world has generally preferred to act from logical consistency or from the high elation of feeling rather than upon daring and clear-sighted experiment. The idea of a social and political opinion which, free from moral prejudice, strains toward scientific proof, as the hypotheses of the physicist strain toward physical laws, is still very new, but it is already playing havoc with the old crusted folkways.

If such opinion is to be this force of the future, there cannot be too much of its guiding thread. Yet it constantly becomes not easier but harder to form valid opinions. We are stunned by the volume of what there is to know in the human world. We are overwhelmed by the mass of sociological data, and brought to despair even more by the great gaps which must be filled. We have every day set before us infinitely more than we can possibly digest. We run the constant risk of missing completely the relevant and the important. Opinion never had a better chance of being based on substrata of quite meaningless facts. The result is often an excessive caution among those whose business it is to know. The universities remain esoteric through the refusal of those who have the wide survey to commit themselves. Those who have the "grounds just short of proof" will not form opinions. Those who will loosely express their opinions have not the grounds. This treason of the intellectual class has neutralized the expected effects of public education. Discussion and universal reading have not really made popular opinion any more intelligent or reliable. They have merely made great masses emotionally articulate, rendered prejudice more vociferous and varied. The need for interpreters, for resolute expressers of opinion, becomes therefore more urgent. Even if real opinion is a Utopian ideal, and no mind can ever make the wide survey and go through the stringent processes necessary to form it, the brave effort must always be made. Its best will not be valueless. To work at breaking up the cake of intellectual custom, at setting the new terms and values that current society needs, at judging events in the light of the larger conceptions of science and the most fruitful social tendencies, will be not to remain entirely futile in the modern world. Quixotic as the enterprise may seem, it is the formation of opinion and not dusty scholarship and solemn cant that will enlist the good-will and best endeavors of those who aim to think worthily.

— *first published in* The New Republic *(September 18, 1915); reprinted by permission of* The New Republic

Solomon Asch was born in Warsaw, Poland, in 1907. He came to the United States in his youth and attended and graduated from the College of the City of New York. Later he studied at Columbia University, where he obtained his M.A. degree in 1928 and his Ph.D. in 1932. He then taught social psychology at Brooklyn College at the New School for Social Research for several years. Since 1947 he has been a professor at Swarthmore College, where he has devoted his attention to teaching and research. He has published a book entitled Social Psychology *and has contributed articles to*

(1907-   )

SOLOMON E. ASCH

periodicals and journals. The essay which follows, "Opinions and Social Pressure," is a clear, readable description of a carefully controlled sociological investigation.

Opinions and Social Pressure

That social influences shape every person's practices, judgments, and beliefs is a truism to which anyone will readily assent. A child masters his "native" dialect down to the finest nuances; a member of a tribe of cannibals accepts cannibalism as altogether fitting and proper. All the social sciences take their departure from the observation of the profound effects that groups exert on their members. For psychologists, group pressure upon the minds of individuals raises a host of questions they would like to investigate in detail.

How, and to what extent, do social forces constrain people's opinions and attitudes? This question is especially pertinent in our day. The same epoch that has witnessed the unprecedented technical extension of communication has also brought into existence the deliberate manipulation of opinion and the "engineering of consent." There are many good reasons why, as citizens and as scientists, we should be concerned with studying the ways in which human beings form their opinions and the role that social conditions play.

Studies of these questions began with the interest in hypnosis aroused by the French physician Jean Martin Charcot (a teacher of Sigmund Freud) toward the end of the nineteenth century. Charcot believed that only hysterical patients could be fully hypnotized, but this view was soon challenged by two other physicians, Hyppolyte Bernheim and A. A. Liébault, who demonstrated that they could put most people under the hypnotic spell. Bernheim proposed that hypnosis was but an extreme form of a normal psychological process which became known as "suggestibility." It was shown that monotonous reiteration of instructions could induce in normal persons in the waking state involuntary bodily changes such as swaying or rigidity of the arms, and sensations such as warmth and odor.

It was not long before social thinkers seized upon these discoveries as a basis for explaining numerous social phenomena, from the spread of opinion to the formation of crowds and the following of leaders. The sociologist Gabriel Tarde summed it all up in the aphorism: "Social man is a somnambulist."

When the new discipline of social psychology was born at the beginning of this century, its first experiments were essentially adaptations of the suggestion demonstration. The technique generally followed a simple plan. The subjects, usually college students, were asked to give their opinions and preferences concerning various matters; some time later they were again asked to state their choices, but now they were also informed of the opinions held by authorities or large groups of their peers on the same matters. (Often the alleged consensus was fictitious.) Most of these studies had substantially the same result: confronted with opinions contrary to their own, many subjects apparently shifted their judgments in the direction of the views of the majorities or the experts. The late psychologist Edward L. Thorndike reported that he had succeeded in modifying the esthetic preferences of adults by this procedure. Other psychologists reported that people's evaluations of the merit of a literary passage could be raised or lowered by ascribing the passage to different authors. Apparently the sheer weight of numbers or authority sufficed to change opinions, even when no arguments for the opinions themselves were provided.

Now the very ease of success in these experiments arouses suspicion. Did the subjects actually change their opinions, or were the experimental victories scored only on paper? On grounds of common sense, one must question whether opinions are generally as watery as these studies indicate. There is some reason to wonder whether it was not the investigators who, in their enthusiasm for a theory, were suggestible, and whether the ostensibly gullible subjects were not providing answers which they thought good subjects were expected to give.

The investigations were guided by certain underlying assumptions, which today are common currency and account for much that is thought and said about the operations of propaganda and public opinion. The assumptions are that people submit uncritically and painlessly to external manipulation by suggestion or prestige, and that any given idea or value can be "sold" or "unsold" without reference to its merits. We should be skeptical, however, of the supposition that the power of social pressure necessarily implies uncritical submission to it: independence and the capacity to rise above group passion are also open to human beings. Further, one may question on psychological grounds whether it is possible as a rule to change a person's judgment of a situation or an object without first changing his knowledge or assumptions about it.

In what follows I shall describe some experiments in an investigation of the effects of group pressure which was carried out recently with the help of a number of my associates. The tests not only demonstrate the operations of group pressure upon individuals but also illustrate a new kind of attack on the problem and some of the more subtle questions that it raises.

A group of seven to nine young men, all college students, are assembled in a classroom for a "psychological experiment" in visual judgment. The experimenter informs them that they will be comparing the lengths of lines. He shows two large white cards. On one is a single vertical black line— the standard whose length is to be matched. On the other card are three vertical lines of various lengths. The subjects are to choose the one that is of the same length as the line on the other card. One of the three actually is of the same length; the other two are substantially different, the difference ranging from three quarters of an inch to an inch and three quarters.

The experiment opens uneventfully. The subjects announce their answers in the order in which they have been seated in the room, and on the first round every person chooses the same matching line. Then a second set of cards is exposed; again the group is unanimous. The members appear ready to endure politely another boring experiment. On the third trial there is an unexpected disturbance. One person near the end of the group disagrees with all the others in his selection of the matching line. He looks surprised, indeed incredulous, about the disagreement. On the following trial he disagrees again, while the others remain unanimous in their choice. The dissenter becomes more and more worried and hesitant as the disagreement continues in succeeding trials; he may pause before announcing his answer and speak in a low voice, or he may smile in an embarrassed way.

What the dissenter does not know is that all the other members of the group were instructed by the experimenter beforehand to give incorrect answers in unanimity at certain points. The single individual who is not a party to this prearrangement is the focal subject of our experiment. He is placed in a position in which, while he is actually giving the correct answers, he finds himself unexpectedly in a minority of one, opposed by a unanimous and arbitrary majority with respect to a clear and simple fact. Upon him we have brought to bear two opposed forces: the evidence of his senses and the unanimous opinion of a group of his peers. Also, he must declare his judgments in public, before a majority which has also stated its position publicly.

The instructed majority occasionally reports correctly in order to reduce the possibility that the naïve subject will suspect collusion against him. (In only a few cases did the subject actually show suspicion; when this happened, the experiment was stopped and the results were not counted.) There are 18 trials in each series, and on 12 of these the majority responds erroneously.

How do people respond to group pressure in this situation? I shall report first the statistical results of a series in which a total of 123 subjects from three institutions of higher learning (not including my own, Swarthmore College) were placed in the minority situation described above.

Two alternatives were open to the subject: he could act independently, repudiating the majority, or he could go along with the majority, repudiating the evidence of his senses. Of the 123 put to the test, a considerable percentage yielded to the majority. Whereas in ordinary circumstances individuals matching the lines will make mistakes less than 1 per cent of the time, under group pressure the minority subjects swung to acceptance of the misleading majority's wrong judgments in 36.8 per cent of the selections.

Of course individuals differed in response. At one extreme, about one quarter of the subjects were completely independent and never agreed with the erroneous judgments of the majority. At the other extreme, some individuals went with the majority nearly all the time. The performances of individuals in this experiment tend to be highly consistent. Those who strike out on the path of independence do not, as a rule, succumb to the majority even over an extended series of trials, while those who choose the path of compliance are unable to free themselves as the ordeal is prolonged.

The reasons for the startling individual differences have not yet been investigated in detail. At this point we can only report some tentative generalizations from talks with the subjects, each of whom was interviewed at the end of the experiment. Among the independent individuals were many who held fast because of staunch confidence in their own judgment. The most significant fact about them was not absence of responsiveness to the majority but a capacity to recover from doubt and to re-establish their equilibrium. Others who acted independently came to believe that the majority was correct in its answers, but they continued their dissent on the simple ground that it was their obligation to call the play as they saw it.

Among the extremely yielding persons we found a group who quickly reached the conclusion: "I am wrong, they are right." Others yielded in order "not to spoil your results." Many of the individuals who went along suspected that the majority were "sheep" following the first responder, or that the majority were victims of an optical illusion; nevertheless, these suspicions failed to free them at the moment of decision. More disquieting were the reactions of subjects who construed their difference from the majority as a sign of some general deficiency in themselves, which at all costs they must hide. On this basis they desperately tried to merge with the majority, not realizing the longer-range consequences to themselves. All the yielding subjects underestimated the frequency with which they conformed.

Which aspect of the influence of a majority is more important—the size of the majority or its unanimity? The experiment was modified to examine this question. In one series the size of the opposition was varied from one to fifteen persons. The results showed a clear trend. When a subject was confronted with only a single individual who contradicted his answers, he was swayed little: he continued to answer independently and correctly in nearly all trials. When the opposition was increased to two, the pressure became substantial: minority subjects now accepted the wrong answer 13.6 per cent of the time. Under the pressure of a majority of three, the subjects' errors jumped to 31.8 per cent. But further increases in the size of the majority apparently did not increase the weight of the pressure substantially. Clearly the size of the opposition is important only up to a point.

Disturbance of the majority's unanimity had a striking effect. In this experiment the subject was given the support of a truthful partner—either another individual who did not know of the prearranged agreement among the rest of the group, or a person who was instructed to give correct answers throughout.

The presence of a supporting partner depleted the majority of much of its power. Its pressure on the dissenting individual was reduced to one fourth: that is, subjects answered incorrectly only one fourth as often as under the pressure of a unanimous majority. The weakest persons did not yield as readily. Most interesting were the reactions to the partner. Generally the feeling toward him was one of warmth and closeness; he was credited with inspiring confidence. However, the subjects repudiated the suggestion that the partner decided them to be independent.

Was the partner's effect a consequence of his dissent, or was it related to his accuracy? We now introduced into the experimental group a person who was instructed to dissent from the majority but also to disagree with the subject. In some experiments the majority was always to choose the worst of the comparison lines and the instructed dissenter to pick the line that was closer to the length of the standard one; in others the majority was consistently intermediate and the dissenter most in error. In this manner we were able to study the relative influence of "compromising" and "extremist" dissenters.

Again the results were clear. When a moderate dissenter is present, the effect of the majority on the subject decreases by approximately one third, and extremes of yielding disappear. Moreover, most of the errors the subjects do make are moderate, rather than flagrant. In short, the dissenter largely controls the choice of errors. To this extent the subjects broke away from the majority even while bending to it.

On the other hand, when the dissenter always chose the line that was more flagrantly different from the standard, the results were of quite a different kind. The extremist dissenter produced a remarkable freeing of the subjects; their errors dropped to only 9 per cent. Furthermore, all the errors were of the moderate variety. We were able to conclude that dissent *per se* increased independence and moderated the errors that occurred, and the direction of dissent exerted consistent effects.

In all the foregoing experiments each subject was observed only in a single setting. We now turned to studying the effects upon a given individual of a change in the situation to which he was exposed. The first experiment examined the consequences of losing or gaining a partner. The instructed partner began by answering correctly on the first six trials. With his support the subject usually resisted pressure from the majority: 18 of 27 subjects were completely independent. But after six trials the partner joined the majority. As soon as he did so, there was an abrupt rise in the subjects' errors. Their submission to the majority was just about as frequent as when the minority subject was opposed by a unanimous majority throughout.

It was surprising to find that the experience of having had a partner and of having braved the majority opposition with him had failed to strengthen the individual's independence. Questioning at the conclusion of the experiment suggested that we had overlooked an important circumstance; namely, the strong specific effect of "desertion" by the partner to the other side. We therefore changed the conditions so that the partner would simply leave the group at the proper point. (To allay suspicion it was announced in advance that he had an appointment with the dean.) In this form of the experiment, the partner's effect outlasted his presence. The errors increased after his departure, but less markedly than after a partner switched to the majority.

In a variant of this procedure the trials began with the majority unanimously giving correct answers. Then they gradually broke away until on the sixth trial the naïve subject was alone and the group unanimously against him. As long as the subject had anyone on his side, he was almost invariably independent, but as soon as he found himself alone, the tendency to conform to the majority rose abruptly.

As might be expected, an individual's resistance to group pressure in these experiments depends to a considerable degree on how wrong the majority is. We varied the discrepancy between the standard line and the other lines systematically, with the hope of reaching a point where the error of the majority would be so glaring that every subject would repudiate it and choose independently. In this we regretfully did not succeed. Even when the difference between the lines was seven inches, there were still some who yielded to the error of the majority.

The study provides clear answers to a few relatively simple questions, and it raises many others that await investigation. We would like to know the degree of consistency of persons in situations which differ in content and structure. If consistency of independence or conformity in behavior is shown to be a fact, how is it functionally related to qualities of character and personality? In what ways is independence related to sociological or cultural conditions? Are leaders more independent than other people, or are they adept at following their followers? These and many other questions may perhaps be answerable by investigations of the type described here.

Life in society requires consensus as an indispensable condition. But consensus, to be productive, requires that each individual contribute independently out of his experience and insight. When consensus comes under the dominance of conformity, the social process is polluted and the individual at the same time surrenders the powers on which his functioning as a feeling and thinking being depends. That we have found the tendency to conformity in our society so strong that reasonably intelligent and well-meaning young people are willing to call white black is a matter of concern. It raises questions about our ways of education and about the values that guide our conduct.

Yet anyone inclined to draw too pessimistic conclusions from this report would do well to remind himself that the capacities for independence are not to be underestimated. He may also draw some consolation from a further observation: those who participated in this challenging experiment agreed nearly without exception that independence was preferable to conformity.

Aldous Huxley was born into a distinguished family: his grandfather, Thomas Henry Huxley, was one of the most famous scientists of the nineteenth century; his father was an outstanding English educator; his brother, Julian Huxley, gained an international reputation as a biologist.

After graduating from Eton, Huxley entered Oxford to study medicine but had to abandon his preparation for a medical career because of failing eyesight. He turned to writing, and during the twenties and thirties published numerous books, including collections of poems, short stories, and essays, as well as such popular novels as Crome Yellow, Antic Hay, and Point Counter Point. Most of his work of this period is satirical; his novels, in particular, present a cynical view of intelligent people leading lives of futility, and substituting sensual pleasures for worthwhile human relationships. In Brave New World (1932) he presents a frightening picture of the "Utopia" we will achieve if we continue to place technological achievement and "standard of living" ahead of human values. In the nineteen-thirties Huxley became interested in the philosophy of mysticism. This interest was expressed in a number of essays and colored his later novels, Eyeless in Gaza and Time Must Have a Stop. In Ape and Essence he forecast the kind of totalitarian world that may emerge after an atomic war.

(1894-1963)

ALDOUS HUXLEY

Time and the Machine

Time, as we know it, is a very recent invention. The modern time-sense is hardly older than the United States. It is a by-product of industrialism—a sort of psychological analogue of synthetic perfumes and aniline dyes.

Time is our tyrant. We are chronically aware of the moving minute hand, even of the moving second hand. We have to be. There are trains to be caught, clocks to be punched, tasks to be done in specified periods, records to be broken by fractions of a second, machines that set the pace and have to be kept up with. Our consciousness of the smallest units of time is now acute. To us, for example, the moment 8:17 a.m. means something—something very important, if it happens to be the starting time of our daily train. To our ancestors, such an odd eccentric instant was without significance—did not even exist. In inventing the locomotive, Watt and Stephenson were part inventors of time.

Another time-emphasizing entity is the factory and its dependent, the office. Factories exist for the purpose of getting certain quantities of goods made in a certain time. The old artisan worked as it suited him; with the result that consumers generally had to wait for the goods they had ordered from him. The factory is a device for making workmen hurry. The machine revolves so often each minute; so many movements have to be made, so many pieces produced each hour. Result: the factory worker (and the same is true, *mutatis mutandis*, of the office worker) is compelled to know time in its smallest fractions. In the hand-work age there was no such compulsion to be aware of minutes and seconds.

Our awareness of time has reached such a pitch of intensity that we suffer acutely whenever our travels take us into some corner of the world where people are not interested in minutes and seconds. The unpunctuality of the Orient, for example, is appalling to those who come freshly from a land of fixed meal-times and regular train services. For a modern American or Englishman, waiting is a psychological torture. An Indian accepts the blank hours with resignation, even with satisfaction. He has not lost the fine art of doing nothing. Our notion of time as a collection of minutes, each of which must be filled with some business or amusements, is wholly alien to the Oriental, just as it was wholly alien to the Greek. For the man who lives in a pre-industrial world, time moves at a slow and easy pace; he does not care about each minute, for the good reason that he has not been made conscious of the existence of minutes.

— *from* <u>*The Olive Tree*</u> *(London, 1936); reprinted by permission of Mrs. Laura Huxley and of Chatto and Windus Limited*

William Faulkner, one of America's greatest and most prolific novelists, was born in New Albany, Mississippi. After serving as a pilot in World War I, he attended the University of Mississippi and then spent several years travelling and working at a variety of jobs before establishing himself as a writer.

Faulkner's novels include <u>Sartoris</u> (1929), <u>The Sound and the Fury</u> (1929), <u>As I Lay Dying</u> (1930), <u>Sanctuary</u> (1931), <u>Light in August</u> (1932), and <u>Requiem for a Nun</u> (1951). The setting of these novels and most of his stories is the imaginary "Yoknapatawpha" County, in Mississippi. Many of the characters described in one story or novel reappear in others, so that the works form a series that presents a realistic picture of decadence and conflict in the deep south. Because Faulkner was continually experimenting with new ways of presenting character and situation his novels are not always easy reading. Perhaps the high-school student's best introduction to his work may be through some of the well-known short stories, such as "The Bear," "Spotted Horses," "Two Soldiers," "A Rose for Emily," "Turnabout," and "Barn Burning."

(1897-1962)

WILLIAM FAULKNER

Speech of Acceptance

UPON THE AWARD OF THE NOBEL PRIZE FOR LITERATURE

delivered in Stockholm on the tenth of December, nineteen hundred fifty

I feel that this award was not made to me as a man, but to my work—a life's work in the agony and sweat of the human spirit, not for glory and least of all for profit, but to create out of the materials of the human spirit something which did not exist before. So this award is only mine in trust. It will not be difficult to find a dedication for the money part of it commensurate with the purpose and significance of its origin. But I would like to do the same with the acclaim too, by using this moment as a pinnacle from which I might be listened to by the young men and women already dedicated to the same anguish and travail, among whom is already that one who will some day stand here where I am standing.

Our tragedy today is a general and universal physical fear so long sustained by now that we can even bear it. There are no longer problems of the spirit. There is only the question: When will I be blown up? Because of this, the young man or woman writing today has forgotten the problems of the human heart in conflict with itself which alone can make good writing because only that is worth writing about, worth the agony and the sweat.

He must learn them again. He must teach himself that the basest of all things is to be afraid; and, teaching himself that, forget it forever, leaving no room in his workshop for anything but the old verities and truths of the

138

heart, the old universal truths lacking which any story is ephemeral and doomed—love and honor and pity and pride and compassion and sacrifice. Until he does so, he labors under a curse. He writes not of love but of lust, of defeats in which nobody loses anything of value, of victories without hope and, worst of all, without pity or compassion. His griefs grieve on no universal bones, leaving no scars. He writes not of the heart but of the glands.

Until he relearns these things, he will write as though he stood among and watched the end of man. I decline to accept the end of man. It is easy enough to say that man is immortal simply because he will endure: that when the last ding-dong of doom has clanged and faded from the last worthless rock hanging tideless in the last red and dying evening, that even then there will still be one more sound: that of his puny inexhaustible voice, still talking. I refuse to accept this. I believe that man will not merely endure: he will prevail. He is immortal, not because he alone among creatures has an inexhaustible voice, but because he has a soul, a spirit capable of compassion and sacrifice and endurance. The poet's, the writer's, duty is to write about these things. It is his privilege to help man endure by lifting his heart, by reminding him of the courage and honor and hope and pride and compassion and pity and sacrifice which have been the glory of his past. The poet's voice need not merely be the record of man, it can be one of the props, the pillars to help him endure and prevail.

Hugh MacLennan was born in Glace Bay, Cape Breton Island, and studied at Dalhousie University. Upon receiving a Rhodes scholarship in 1929, he went to Oriel College, Oxford, and from there to Princeton where he graduated with a Ph.D. degree. He taught classics for a time at Lower Canada College. His first novel, Barometer Rising, was published in 1941 (and has subsequently been translated into French). It is centred around the Halifax Explosion of 1917, which MacLennan witnessed as a boy. In 1943 MacLennan was awarded a Guggenheim fellowship in creative writing, whereupon he spent a few years in New York. Since 1951 he has been on the staff of McGill University.

MacLennan's work has received wide recognition in Canada. Four of his novels, including The Watch that Ends the Night (1959), and two collections of essays, Cross-Country (1949) and Thirty and Three (1955), have won Governor General's awards; in 1952 he received the Lorne Pierce Medal for his contribution to Canadian literature. His most recent novel is An Orange from Portugal (1964).

In much of his earlier writing MacLennan concerns himself with interpreting the Canadian character and consciousness. Two Solitudes (1945), a novel, deals with the relationship between French and English, Canada's predominating cultures. His more recent novels explore themes that are perhaps more universal. In the essay that follows, MacLennan considers the impact of a social conscience on creativity. It might be interesting to compare his point of view with that expressed by Faulkner.

(1907-   )

HUGH MacLENNAN

The Shadow of Captain Bligh

Not long ago, in the same evening, I listened to my gramophone recording of Haydn's *Mass for St. Cecilia* and then went upstairs and began rereading the account of the mutiny on H.M.S. *Bounty* as written by Nordhoff and Hall. The grand cadences of the Mass kept sounding through my mind, and every now and then I stopped reading to let them swell and subside. I was rereading the book for a purpose and I didn't feel I could put it down. But the counterpoint made me realize with a sensation of shock that Joseph Haydn and Captain Bligh were contemporaries, that the society that had produced and honored the one was the same society that had employed and respected the other.

Haydn's *Mass for St. Cecilia*, which was partially lost until Dr. Brand recovered it little more than a decade ago, and which hardly anyone had heard performed until it appeared recently in a recording of the Haydn Society, is certainly one of the most sublime works the human spirit has ever created. It seems to me worth all the music composed since the death of

Beethoven. Beethoven himself was never able to sustain the power that is manifest here, for his struggle with himself and his medium was too great. Haydn's *Mass*, like the greatest work of Shakespeare, is at once majestic and intimate. Above all it seems effortless, and its joy and triumph are so breathtaking that no one who is moved by music can easily listen to it without reflecting that our modern world has produced no creative genius with his originality, his joyousness, or his power.

Yet Haydn was not unique in his time. His career overlapped those of Bach, Handel, Mozart, and Beethoven. Though his age acclaimed him a master, it occurred to nobody in the eighteenth century to think it miraculous that he was able to compose those immensely complex works, some of great length, in so short a time. The best of his contemporaries were equally prolific and worked with equal speed. Handel composed *The Messiah* in a few weeks and Mozart wrote one of his most famous symphonies in a few days. Compared to these eighteenth-century masters, a modern creative artist moves at a snail's pace. Our most famous poets will die leaving behind only a slim body of published verse. The average modern novelist takes from two to three years to write a single good novel. Our musicians—men like Sibelius, Stravinsky, and Vaughan Williams—have together, in their long lives, equalled only a fraction of Haydn's output.

How lucky Haydn was to have lived before the radio and the telephone, before civic societies which would have made exorbitant and unavoidable demands on his time and energy, before publicity and interviewers and income tax and traffic horns and metropolitan dailies—to have lived, in short, before the age of distraction.

But *Mutiny on the Bounty* reminded me of the other side of the eighteenth century. The very fact of Captain Bligh implies that the forces which have made ours an age of distraction are far subtler and less avoidable than technical innovations like the telephone and the radio. *Mutiny on the Bounty* should be required reading for anyone who is apt, like myself, to be romantic about past ages and to decry his own. For Captain Bligh was just as typical of the eighteenth century as Haydn was. When I bow before Haydn I must remember that Haydn accepted without question and apparently without remorse the fact that he lived in a world that contained Captain Bligh.

Nothing Mickey Spillane has ever written can be compared in horror to some of the factual scenes in *Mutiny on the Bounty*. Few passages in literature describe more revolting episodes than those of the *Bounty* sailors being seized in the gangway and flogged until the flesh hung in strips from their backs. With our modern knowledge of neurology, we know that the agonies of these poor creatures did not end when the boatswain's mate ceased swinging the cat. Such beatings damaged the nerve roots along the spine and condemned the victims to permanent suffering. What makes those scenes of torture so unbearable to think about is the added realization that they were not sporadic, were not the offshoots of a psychopathic movement like Naziism, but were standard practice in one of the most stable and reflective societies that ever existed. Captain Bligh's cruelty had the weight and approval of his entire society behind it. When the mutineers were later court-martialled, the court had no interest in determining whether Bligh had been cruel or not. It was interested solely in whether the accused had obeyed to the letter the harsh laws of the British Navy.

Haydn, Bach, Handel, and Mozart, sublime spirits full of mercy, with sensibilities exquisitely delicate, knew that men like Bligh were the mainstays of the societies they inhabited. Yet this knowledge which to us would be a shame, felt personally, seldom if ever troubled their dreams or ruffled their serenity. The humanitarianism that disturbed Beethoven a generation later had not dawned when Haydn wrote the *Mass for St. Cecilia*.

Haydn reached his prime in the last moments when it was possible for a creative artist to mind his own business in the sense that his conscience could remain untroubled by the sufferings of the unfortunate. If sailors were flogged to death and peasants had no rights, if a neighboring country was ruined by famine or pestilence, if laws were unjust or princes cruel, none was Haydn's affair. He was compelled to no empathy in the suffering of others as modern artists are.

It is this awareness of personal responsibility for the welfare of strangers that makes uneasy all men of imagination today, that troubles their work and makes much of it seem tortured, that frustrates it too, for seldom can a modern man of creative imagination do anything concrete to change the world he lives in.

Responsible only to himself, to his family, and to his God, Haydn enjoyed a freedom few artists have known since. The result was as glorious as it is inimitable. It is on most of his successors that the shadow of Captain Bligh has fallen and remained.

As Haydn represents the spiritual grandeur of the eighteenth-century imagination, Bligh represents its irresponsibility. In Bligh's own words, it was only through fear and cruelty that the stupid, the weak, the incompetent, the ignorant, and the unfortunate could be ruled and compelled to do what their masters considered to be their duty. Unless they were so compelled, the supporters of the system argued, there could be no fineness, no spiritual grandeur, no great literature or beautiful buildings, no masses for St. Cecilia. Civilization, as men of Haydn's day conceived it, could not exist if it yielded to the promptings of a social conscience.

When we realize this it becomes easier to reconcile ourselves to the fact that the world we live in is producing no more Haydns or Mozarts. In the nineteenth century, men of imagination turned their attention to the miseries of the world they saw about them, accepted responsibility for it, and forever lost the peace and concentration of spirit which enabled the Haydns and

Mozarts to devote the full force of their genius to the realization of the gifts God had given them.

Could a modern artist witness a public flogging and then go home and compose exquisite music? Could he even live quietly under a régime that permitted such atrocities and retain his own respect and that of others?

Merely to ask such questions is to answer them. Musicians who took no more active part in the Hitler régime than perform for a Nazi audience have had to spend years as outcasts before western society would accept them again. The social conscience of today demands the service of every artist alive, and does not forgive him if he refuses it.

On the other hand western society did not make outcasts of the physicists, chemists, and engineers who served Hitler. Until very recently science reserved for itself the same mental freedom that art enjoyed in Haydn's day. If politicians or monsters used the work of science for evil purposes, the scientists felt no personal responsibility. Enjoying such peace of mind, physicists and chemists have been able to devote the full force of their intellects to their work, and so their work has been more impressive than that of the artists who were their contemporaries. No wonder our age, when it looks for a genius to match Bach or Haydn, does not even stop to search among the ranks of the artists. It picks Einstein.

But when the atomic bomb fell on Hiroshima any number of scientists succumbed to a social conscience as the artists had done long ago. Einstein, Oppenheimer, and hundreds of others were overcome with a Hamlet-like self-questioning. If our world lasts long enough it will be interesting to see whether science in the next generation will be as original and productive as it has been in the last three. For a conscience, as Shakespeare knew when he created Hamlet, inhibits action and beclouds genius. Our collective conscience may not have made the modern artist a coward, but it has certainly made him a prisoner.

Consider in contrast to Haydn the life of Albert Schweitzer. Schweitzer began as a musician, and had he lived in the eighteenth century there is no knowing what masterpieces he might have composed. But his conscience would not permit him to devote his entire life to music, so he studied theology and became a minister of the Gospel. Then his conscience told him that preaching was not enough, so he studied medicine and became a doctor. His conscience then informed him that it was self-indulgent to practise medicine in a comfortable European city while there were millions in the world without medical care of any kind. So Schweitzer took his gifts to one of the most primitive parts of Africa. There he has lived and worked ever since, among men so elemental that they can know nothing of Bach or Haydn and cannot even guess at the greatness of the strange healer who came to help them.

Albert Schweitzer will die leaving behind him no tangible or audible monument, no record of objective achievement beyond a few books which are mere by-products of his life and interests. His enormous powers have been spread so widely in the service of others that neither as a musician, nor as a theologian, nor as a doctor-scientist, has his work, in itself, been such as to ensure his immortality. An earlier age would have said that Schweitzer had squandered his gifts on savages. But our age, rightly or wrongly, acclaims him as one of its noblest representatives because his life has translated into action, as hardly any other life has done, the highest aspirations of our social conscience.

No other modern artist I know of has made the total sacrifice of his talents that Schweitzer made; yet no modern artist (musician or poet or even the great individualist Picasso) has been undisturbed by the social conscience of our day.

Critics who argue that the subject-matter of modern art is proof of the decadence of modern society don't really understand what they are talking about. Art has always been a reflection of the aspirations and obsessions of its time and the art of today is no exception. If it is haunted and distracted, if it is often ugly and even horrifying, it does not mean that the artists themselves are worse men than Haydn was. It means only that they have not refused, as Haydn did, to accept responsibility for Captain Bligh. For all its horrors, the twentieth century is better than the eighteenth; no politician or dictator who has tried to defy its conscience has been able, in the end, to succeed.

Some time in the future, art may reflect the tranquillity that Haydn knew. If it does so, it will not be because those artists of the future are likely to be abler men than artists of today. It will happen because, after this age of transition, the shadow of Captain Bligh has been removed from the whole world.

— from Thirty and Three (Toronto, Macmillan, 1954); reprinted by permission of Hugh MacLennan and of The Macmillan Company of Canada Limited

Alphabetical index — authors and titles